# Change in Educational Policy

# Change in Educational Policy

SELF-STUDIES IN SELECTED
COLLEGES AND UNIVERSITIES

by *Dwight R. Ladd*

Professor, The Whittemore School of Business and Economics,
University of New Hampshire

with commentary by *Katharine McBride*

---

A General Report Prepared for
*The Carnegie Commission on Higher Education*

MC GRAW-HILL BOOK COMPANY
New York   St. Louis   San Francisco   Düsseldorf
London   Sydney   Toronto   Mexico   Panama

*The Carnegie Commission on Higher Education,
1947 Center Street, Berkeley, California 94704,
has sponsored preparation of this report as a
part of a continuing effort to obtain and present
significant information for public discussion.
The views expressed are those of the author.*

CHANGE IN EDUCATIONAL POLICY

*Self-studies in Selected Colleges and Universities*

Library of Congress catalog card number 76-118785

123456789MAMM79876543210
10013

# Foreword

During the 1960s, some colleges and universities in the United States became aware of the need for changes in fundamental policies. Even institutions that were well known for academic experimentation and flexibility became involved in thorough self-examination to discover weaknesses in educational endeavors and to prescribe cures for whatever ailments were diagnosed. Among the institutions that undertook such studies were the University of California at Berkeley, the University of New Hampshire, the University of Toronto, Swarthmore College, Wesleyan University, Michigan State University, Duke University, Brown University, Stanford University, Columbia College, and the University of California at Los Angeles. As Dwight Ladd points out in his excellent review of these and other efforts, the attempts to achieve change generally were made in accordance with a collegial tradition that assumed that responsible members of the academic community would set individual and departmental interests aside and accept changes clearly needed for the good of the entire institution.

One of the problems often encountered was that the weaknesses discovered by the groups conducting the examinations were often long-standing and long deplored:

- There was ready agreement that the quality of teaching should be improved.

- Advising procedures should be more effective.

- Opportunities for members of the college community to work together and develop natural and constructive relationships should be expanded at all ranks and levels.

- Curricula should be more flexible.

- Grading should be less threatening and should give students a better sense of their standing, strengths, and shortcomings.

The committees reviewing educational policies had little difficulty discovering these problems and some of them proposed imaginative solutions. But the task of converting what many people regarded as platitudes into policies and then converting policies into practice has required tens of thousands of man-hours from the schedules of busy professors, and the results of their labors are, as yet, hard to assess. Institutions with a record of innovation extending over many years needed relatively modest change to stay in the vanguard of educational progress. At institutions clearly in need of considerable reform, achievement of modest change seemed little better than failure.

Professor Ladd gives us an abundance of useful information about specific educational policy issues. He also provides useful analyses of the ways in which the policy committees were appointed and pursued their assignments. Inevitably such an analysis leads to the larger issue of how institutions of higher learning have to be organized to change when demands and conditions warrant change. Professor Ladd addresses this larger issue in a provocative final chapter.

*Clark Kerr*
*Chairman*
*The Carnegie Commission*
*on Higher Education*

*June, 1970*

# Contents

# 1. *Introduction*

In spite of much contemporary rhetoric to the contrary, colleges and universities do change, and most past change has come about through the orderly — albeit leisurely — process of self-study, debate, and consensus, rather than through confrontation. Critical questioning of the state of the universities did not begin on the steps of Sproul Hall. On the other hand, lately there has been a widespread sense of urgency about change in the universities because the overall environment of higher education has been changing with such astonishing rapidity. Enrollment and costs have grown at a breakneck pace. The background and outlook of many students have changed markedly. There has been a knowledge explosion, and an Academic Revolution has occurred. Each of these phenomena influences, or should influence, the educational policies and processes of the universities. It is because many have felt that educational policies have not responded sufficiently to these rapid and sweeping changes in the environment that pressures for action have increased. (Much of the campus turmoil which has occurred since about 1966 has been related to the war in Vietnam and the draft and to the enrollment and treatment of black students. No doubt these have increased the tempo of demands for educational reform, but the latter have existed independently.)

In this atmosphere of pressure for change, a number of colleges and universities, since the early 1960s, have undertaken wide-ranging reviews of educational policies and processes. There are many indications of intentions that these reviews should lead to changes of consequence. As President John Hannah put it when inaugurating such a study at Michigan State, "Reforms far more basic than the juggling of existing course offerings and novel ways to expose more students to the traditional patterns of teaching and evaluation may be needed."[1]

---

[1] See item 6 on p. 4.

It would be an overstatement to say that these several studies constitute a movement, but it is the case that a tremendous amount of energy and time has gone into them in institutions as diverse and as generally influential as Duke and Berkeley or Swarthmore and Michigan State. Consequently, the Carnegie Commission on Higher Education and I believed that a review of these studies and how they were conducted might illuminate some important questions about contemporary higher education: What does a fairly large and diverse group of university people see as present-day educational policy problems? What do they think might be done about them? How effective are the traditional processes for bringing about major policy changes within the university? Consequently, in spite of a somewhat "Alice in Wonderland" quality in the idea of a study of studies, it seemed appropriate to undertake just that. This volume is a report on that study. It describes and evaluates both the educational policy changes proposed in a number of institutions between 1965 and 1969 and the processes by which these proposed changes were developed and disposed of by the institutions involved.

The decision to undertake this study was made in the spring of 1968—just prior to the Columbia crisis—and was carried on during what must surely have been the most tumultuous year in the history of American higher education. Whether or not the turmoil will continue—and writing now in the early summer of 1969 it is difficult not to feel that this quiet summer is only an interlude—the recent state of the university world requires bearing several important cautions and qualifications in mind.

For one thing, the pace of change is so rapid that it is difficult to put these studies in the context of their time—even though their time was only a year or two ago. For example, most of the studies reviewed made little or no mention of university government and especially of student participation in that government. Perhaps one can criticize the failure of those preparing the studies to foresee that this would become almost an overriding issue in the universities, but until the gift of great foresight is more widely distributed, it seems more equitable to evaluate these studies in terms of the issues considered vital at the time they were done.

Second, the fact that so much has happened in so short a time makes it difficult to avoid the use of hindsight. As in our society as a whole, the phenomenon of rising expectations may be at work in university affairs. Changes were made as a result of these studies, but continuing unrest indicates that these changes were not enough, even though at the time they were made, many of them were marked departures from the previous policies or practices of the institution.

Finally, there may be a sense of unreality about the whole thing. All these studies used the traditional liberal and collegial process of study, analysis, and debate leading to decisions based on general acceptability. These processes assume that the university is, in fact, a liberal and collegial place, a place where change results from reasoned and reasonable discourse among peers. As one looks back, again from the perspective of the summer of 1969, on the instances where the university has become a radical and divided place, a place where force has come to replace discourse, one must wonder whether our educational institutions are not in the process of becoming very, very different from what most of us have always known, or at least thought, them to be. The several studies, and this report on them, assumed a context of evolutionary change within a framework of traditional objectives and structure. It is at least possible that the context has been disappearing—even during the so short period when these studies were made.

**SOURCES AND PROCEDURES**    There are two principal sources for the descriptions and analyses which follow: texts of reports prepared by individuals or committees at a number of colleges and universities and data I gathered from those institutions about the origins, conduct, and ultimate disposition of the studies. The reports and institutions which form the principal base for this study are the following:

1    *Education at Berkeley,* by the Select Committee on Education, Academic Senate, University of California, Berkeley. March, 1966 (Berk.)[2]

2    *Toward Unity from Diversity,* by the University-wide Educational Policies Committee, University of New Hampshire. February, 1967 (NH)

3    *Undergraduate Instruction in Arts and Sciences,* by the Presidential Advisory Committee on Undergraduate Instruction, Faculty of Arts and Sciences, University of Toronto. July, 1967 (Tor.)

4    *Critique of a College,* by the Commission on Educational Policy, Swarthmore College. November, 1967 (Sw.)

5    *The Study of Educational Policies and Programs at Wesleyan,* Wesleyan University. May, 1968 (Wes.)

[2] The letters in parentheses after each listing will be used as the reference whenever the particular report is cited.

6 *Improving Undergraduate Education,* by the Committee on Undergraduate Education, Michigan State University. October, 1967 (MS)

7 *Varieties of Learning Experience,* by the Subcommittee on Curriculum, Undergraduate Faculty Council, Duke University. March, 1968 (Duke)

8 *Interim Report and Recommendations,* by the Special Committee on Educational Principles, Brown University. April, 1969 (Br.)

9 *Study of Education at Stanford,* by the Steering Committee of the Study of Education at Stanford, Stanford University. November, 1968, *et seq.* (Stan.)

10 *The Reforming of General Education: The Columbia College Experience in Its National Setting,* by Daniel Bell. Columbia University Press, New York, 1966 (Bell)

11 *Report,* by the Committee on Academic Innovation and Development, Academic Senate, University of California, Los Angeles. November, 1967 (UCLA)

Certain colleges and universities not included in this list were visited, and reports from a number of institutions not visited were reviewed. The essential basis for the report, however, is the 11 institutions listed. These are not presented as a scientifically drawn sample of American colleges and universities. There are, for example, no avowedly experimental colleges, no women's colleges, and no black colleges. It can be said, however, that all these institutions are a part of the mainstream of American higher education. Some are very large and some are quite small. Some are public and some are private. There are — to use David Riesman's handy phrase — both Hertz and Avis universities. It is these four- (or more) year institutions which have set much of the tone for American higher education (Riesman, 1956). The sources used here are not necessarily representative in the formal sense, but they are typical.[3]

This review is based primarily on the reports and related documents and on interviews. The reports were studied and catalogs and

[3] The inclusion of the University of Toronto was initially intended to provide a possible contrast. While English-Canadian universities have always had many close contacts with American institutions, they have retained strong ties with the British tradition. In addition, Canadian society has not been tortured in recent years by such issues as civil rights or the war in Vietnam. However, after reviewing the Toronto material, the reader will surely agree that neither the student revolt nor the Academic Revolution has been confined by international boundaries. Perhaps this should be no surprise. After all, Marshall McLuhan first proclaimed the existence of the "global village" from the Toronto campus.

other descriptive material were reviewed before visits to the campuses were made. Each campus was visited once, most a second time. During these visits as many as possible of the people directly involved in the conduct of the study were interviewed. Other persons known to have strongly favored or opposed the recommendations were also interviewed, as were the principal administrators responsible for initiating and implementing the study. In most, but not all, cases some students were interviewed. The interviews were based on the following questions:

1 *Origins of the study.* From what events or individuals or groups did the pressure for undertaking the study come? Was the study authorized and initiated by administrative officers, by faculty senate or similar body or some other group? To what extent was the ultimate disposition of the study considered prior to beginning it?

2 *Makeup of the study group.* How and by whom was the study group selected? What factors governed the choice of people?

3 *Processes of the study.* How did the study group work? To what extent were others in the institution (faculty, students, administration) involved? How were they involved? To what extent and how were resources from outside the university involved?

4 *Consideration and implementation.* What were the processes utilized in obtaining consideration of, and action upon, the recommendations? Was someone given responsibility to follow through the legislative process? If so, who? What recommendations were generally accepted or rejected? (Is there a pattern of acceptance and rejection among the institutions studied?) What people or groups generally responded favorably or unfavorably to the recommendations? To what extent, if any, was there a connection between the origin of the study and its eventual adoption or rejection?

In addition, the interviews usually included questions about the intent of specific proposals in the particular report and about the relationship of these proposals to the realities of the institution.

In arranging for my visits I was, of course, somewhat restricted by the interview schedule which my specific host had arranged, though it was quite clear that in all cases a serious attempt was made to ensure that I got a representative cross section of campus opinion. Though my host was usually identified in some way with the local study, I met, on every campus, with persons who were not sympathetic toward at least some aspects of the study. Furthermore, I was often led, by interviewees, to others who were not on my list and who had differing views of what had taken place. Also, in a great many cases, I was able to arrange interviews with persons whom I know or to whom I had been directed by an acquaintance. Campus visits were invariably followed by correspondence with one or more of those whom I had interviewed, and each of the case studies included here was reviewed by at least one person at the institution involved. Before I began this study, I spent nearly two years acting as chairman of the study committee at the University of New Hampshire. While this experience gave me no special expertise as a researcher, it did give me some feeling for the process that I was investigating.

**THE PLAN OF THE REPORT**

Part 1 includes nine case studies which describe in some detail the entire process of each study from its origins to either its ostensible conclusion or the present time and, in Chapter 11, two abbreviated case studies. The order in which the cases are presented is based on the date when each study began, though for the most part this is not significant since the studies cover a very short time span. Each of the case studies includes a short summary of the specific recommendations made in the report.

Part 2 includes (in Chapters 12 to 16) discussions of the educational policy proposals made in the studies, with emphasis given to the reasoning behind them. It is only moderately Procrustean to discuss these reports collectively in terms of major issues—teaching, general education, environment, and so on—for, with remarkably few exceptions, the reports have identified the same problems and have proposed the same general solutions.

As suggested earlier, the institutions from which these reports came do not constitute a true sample of American higher education. The reports do, however, represent directly the thinking of roughly 100 members (and indirectly of a great many more) of generally important and influential institutions. It seems reasonable to assume that what these reports identify as educational problems will be problems in a great many more institutions and that the solutions they propose would be typical of those proposed elsewhere. One's confidence in the validity of this assumption is enhanced by the very considerable similarity between the several reports noted above. While all deal with some issues which are essentially local, the primary concerns are the same in almost all the reports, and the approaches to these issues are remarkably similar.

Two limitations should be borne in mind. In the first place, the discussions in these chapters are about undergraduate education.

Several of the committees studied only undergraduate education, and most of the others gave attention to the content and processes of graduate study only as they might impinge on undergraduate education. This is not to say that graduate study is an unimportant part of American higher education—especially in some of the institutions included here. It is to say that most appear to have shared the view of the New Hampshire study "that the undergraduate student body is that part of the university community most demanding of attention at the moment" (NH, p.2).

Second, the review presented here is not of the scorekeeping variety ("Seven institutions recommended a required year of physical education, and five did not."). For one thing, there are nearly always enough differences in detail to make such comparisons impossible without almost stultifying qualification. More importantly, the broad, overall thrust of the recommendations and the reasoning behind them will, I believe, give a much better overview of the thinking of those who make the educational policies and who organize the processes of our colleges and universities.

Chapter 17 returns to the cases as the basis for a general analysis and evaluation of the processes by which the studies were started, carried on, and disposed of by the various decision-making agencies involved.

One would like to be able to conclude from such analyses that certain processes or techniques generally ensured a "successful" study and that "failures" could be attributed to certain actions or omissions. Unfortunately, this is not entirely possible to do because, generally speaking, these studies cannot be assessed in terms of success or failure except in an impressionistic way.

One difficulty is that a history of legislative actions can be remarkably inaccurate. A number of policies and procedures intended to improve academic advising, for example, may be passed by overwhelming margins, but unless large numbers of individual faculty members change their attitudes about this activity significantly, no real change will occur—votes notwithstanding. Conversely, if a recommendation for a program of freshman tutorials is not accepted by the institution as a whole, but is subsequently implemented—even in an experimental way—by one of the institution's subunits, it is not evident that the original proposal really failed. Furthermore, reliance on a legislative record becomes more uncertain as time passes. No university is static—least of all during the past two or three years—and some change takes place continually. When something proposed by one of these reports is brought up and adopted two years later, it is difficult to be sure of a cause-and-effect relationship.

A second difficulty is that even if the legislative record mirrored the real results, one would still have to accommodate the fact that the impact of a proposal on different institutions varies substantially. For example, similar proposals for small freshman classes were made at Brown and New Hampshire, but the impact of adoption would be much greater at New Hampshire, which has about twice as many freshmen, a somewhat lower teacher-student ratio, and significantly less money. Similarly, at both Wesleyan and Toronto, elimination of all specific curriculum requirements was proposed, but the impact of acceptance would be quite different, since Toronto had very rigid requirements, while Wesleyan had hardly any to begin with. In other words, success must be qualified by the relative ease with which it can be achieved.

On the other hand, each case study does provide a basis for an impressionistic evaluation as to whether or not a particular campus was stirred to some fundamental reexamination. In varying degrees, each of the reports was intended to be inspirational. Addressed, in most cases, to fellow faculty members and administrators, each report called for major changes in basic attitudes about education and about the institution. As a member of one study group wrote, "The report was intended to have some of the passion that moves men off their behinds, to 'raise some standards to which the good and the honest might repair!'"[4] It is obviously not possible, in a study such as this, to attempt an objective measurement of whether or not men were, in fact, moved off their behinds. On the other hand, in such a case subjective conclusions based on interviews with several persons on a campus while events are taking place or are fresh in memory may be just as reliable. In any event, such impressions are a part of the limited conclusions which are made here about the success of the studies.

In reviewing the individual case studies, the reader should keep in mind that all that is being attempted here is the description and

---

[4] It is characteristic of virtually all the study groups that they became imbued with a sense of urgency and of a mission to lead change. While John Gardner was never quoted, as far as I can recall, the idea of self-renewal obviously took hold within most of the study groups. This suggests, perhaps, that the universities would benefit greatly from having groups such as these more or less continuously in session.

evaluation of a particular series of events in the university in question. There is no basis in these data for an evaluation of the institution in any other context. Obviously, the events surrounding any one of these studies were influenced by the particular character of, and the personalities within, the particular institution, but except as is necessary to explain the facts, these are not commented upon here. In short, the fact that a particular study appears generally to have been successful or unsuccessful should not, and does not, lead to a conclusion that the institution is somehow "good" or "bad."

On the whole the educational policy changes proposed vary considerably in their venturesomeness, and they often seem to speak indirectly—if at all—to the deep malaise which presently affects so much of American higher education. Nevertheless, if the proposals were to be adopted by the institutions concerned, truly consequential changes would be made in the educational policies of those institutions. Generally speaking, the cases demonstrate that the proposals developed in the studies became less venturesome or simply disappeared as they passed through the various centers of decision making except where some form of countervailing power was present. Daniel Bell (1966, p. 65) observed that " . . . it is more the academic habit to deal with ideological questions than with organizational difficulties." The cases support Bell's conclusions quite directly, and more importantly they suggest the results of this "academic habit." The ability of our colleges and universities to respond to a need for change—except when faced with severe pressure or the threat of such pressure—is frighteningly limited.

The 11 case studies which follow are the basis for the analysis and commentary which make up the second part of this report. Each of the case studies has certain unique features and points of intrinsic interest. The reader who is or is about to become involved in an institutional policy study will undoubtedly wish to review all of them. The general reader may well be ready to move on to the chapters of analysis and commentary after sampling some of the cases. He may safely do so.

# Part One
## Selected Case Studies

# 2. University of California at Berkeley

## Education at Berkeley

"Berkeley" has become almost a household word since 1964.[1] Many books, countless articles, and no doubt miles of news columns have been written about that troubled place, and the query "What more can one possibly say?" is immensely relevant. It is probably true that I can, in fact, add nothing to what has been said elsewhere, but there are certain facts about the Muscatine report which are important within the context of this review of educational policy studies. They will be briefly presented here to round out the present study. Unless some secondary source is specifically identified, the data on which the following case study is based come entirely from interviews with persons who were members of the Berkeley faculty, administration, or student body at the time of the events described.

Berkeley is the senior unit in the University of California. In 1965, it enrolled about 27,000 students, of whom nearly 17,000 were undergraduates. Over 12,000 of the latter were enrolled in the College of Letters and Science. Berkeley also had undergraduate colleges or schools of agriculture, business administration, chemistry, criminology, engineering, environmental design, and forestry. The Berkeley faculty numbered about 1,700 and was supplemented by some 1,200 teaching assistants. In addition to the undergraduate schools and colleges, Berkeley had schools of law and of education which enrolled only postbaccalaureate stu-

---

[1] The reader is asked to bear in mind that the events described here occurred between the spring of 1965 and the fall of 1966. Since that time, many things have occurred at Berkeley which are familiar to all. But to repeat the caution put forward in the "Introduction," we are not here discussing individual institutions as institutions. We are simply describing and discussing a specific event which has occurred in a number of institutions.

dents and maintained some 50 research institutes. Berkeley has long maintained an international reputation as a center of excellence in graduate study and research, and in general its faculty has reflected these professional interests rather than an interest in the general education usually associated with undergraduates.

In 1965, the formulation of educational policy at Berkeley was largely in the hands of the Academic Senate. Officially, all those who had held faculty rank at Berkeley for more than two years were eligible to vote in the Academic Senate, but as a practical matter, only a relatively small number of faculty members attended senate meetings. In large measure, this same relatively small group provided membership for the important standing committees of the senate. Special committees were invariably created by vote of the Academic Senate, and membership of all committees was selected by its Committee on Committees. In short, the Berkeley faculty—or at least that portion of the faculty which was politically active—had a great deal of power in terms of setting educational policy. However, in response to the turmoil and shock that accompanied the Free Speech Movement, which erupted in late 1964, the Academic Senate created an Emergency Executive Committee with rather sweeping temporary powers. That committee played an important role in the establishment of the Select Committee on Education, or the Muscatine Committee, as it is widely known.

**ORIGIN OF THE STUDY** In an immediate sense, the Muscatine Committee arose out of the Free Speech Movement, which developed in the autumn of 1964. Originally concerned only with essentially political issues, the Free Speech Movement began to involve itself with educational matters which were of direct and continuing concern to a very much larger number of students. As a result, many of the things which made students discontented with their lives and their education at Berkeley came into the open. As one faculty member put it, "The FSM caused many faculty members to see themselves for the first time."

Berkeley's educational policies had not been static in a literal sense. The entire University of California had recently converted to the quarter system—an innovation pushed by President Kerr partly in the hope that such a major structural change would bring about other changes in curriculum and pedagogy. The Tussman Program—an integrated, interdisciplinary program of study for a small number of freshmen and sophomores—had started in the fall of 1964, though hardly with any widespread enthusiasm on the part of the faculty as a whole. Many individual departments and individual faculty members had been engaged in experimentation and innovation. Nevertheless, the university as a whole was not characterized by a widespread interest in undergraduate education. As one long-time faculty member who was active in university affairs put it, "There was a degree of validity in the claim that educational reform was needed." Many, though not all, faculty members who were concerned about educational reform had allied themselves with the Free Speech Movement.

On March 1, 1965, Chancellor Martin Meyerson addressed the Academic Senate on the subject of educational reform and called for the creation of a special commission on the state of education at Berkeley. During the preceding weeks, some members of the Emergency Executive Committee had been urging that the faculty take the initiative in bringing about educational reform, and after the chancellor's speech they were able to get the committee to draft a resolution calling for the creation of a Select Committee on Education at Berkeley. This resolution passed the Academic Senate on March 8, 1965, but by a rather close vote—an indication, no doubt, that apart from the crisis, there was not widespread concern for change in educational policies at Berkeley.

**SELECTION OF THE COMMITTEE** Committee members were chosen by the Emergency Executive Committee after widespread consultation with the chancellor, other faculty members, and students. (The issue of student membership on the committee did not arise in any formal way.) The committee was clearly intended to be representative of the spectrum of political and educational persuasions present on the Berkeley faculty. A couple of the members were generally identified as radicals or reformers, while some others were clearly more conservative members of the Berkeley establishment. Professor Charles Muscatine, chosen as chairman, was described by one faculty member as being "politically, educationally, and generally prominent," and all indications are that he was widely respected by almost everyone. Professor Muscatine suggested that committee members were chosen from among the "few members of the Berkeley faculty who had shown any egregious interest in education." In any case, while the committee was formed largely in response to the extreme pressure for change, not all its members could be expected to push for or support sweeping change.

WORK OF THE
COMMITTEE The committee began its work in mid-April. Most of the members knew only one or two other members, and several had had relatively little experience with major committee work. Consequently, a number of the early meetings were devoted to identifying problems and getting acquainted. The committee, under the leadership of the chairman, concerned itself with specific issues rather than with trying to develop a mutually acceptable educational philosophy.

The committee was given funds by the chancellor, which made it possible to pay faculty members and graduate and undergraduate students for doing research into a number of specific questions. In addition, some volunteer work was given to the committee. (For example, the chapter in the report on teaching assistants is based largely on research done by the committee's staff.) Written submissions were asked for and received in connection with a number of specific topics, and meetings or hearings were held with a number of individuals or groups.

Some members of the committee stated that much of the research had relatively little effect on the committee's thinking because the results were not available until too late in the committee's work. These committee members felt that many of the meetings with other individuals and groups were of limited value relative to the time they took. Other committee members suggested that these meetings and much of the research were of value, and all agreed that the use of graduate and undergraduate students on the committee's staff did serve to keep committee members in touch with student

**TABLE 1** *Membership of the Select Committee on Education, University of California at Berkeley*

| Name and rank | Field | Age group* | Years at Berkeley | Degrees from Berkeley |
|---|---|---|---|---|
| Richard Herr, professor | History | 42–49 | 5 | None |
| David Krech, professor | Psychology | 50–57 | 18 | Ph.D. |
| Leo Lowenthal, professor | Sociology | Over 58 | 9 | None |
| Charles Muscatine, professor | English | 42–49 | 17 | None |
| Roderic Park, associate professor | Botany | 34–41 | 5 | None |
| George Pimental, professor | Chemistry | 42–49 | 16 | A.B., Ph.D. |
| Samuel Schaaf, professor | Mechanical engineering | 42–49 | 18 | A.B., Ph.D. |
| Peter Scott, assistant professor | Speech | 34–41 | 4 | None |
| Theodore Vermeulen, professor | Chemical engineering | 42–49 | 18 | None |

*Ages and years at the institution are given as of the time the committee was first convened.

views. Similarly, all the meetings and hearings served to keep the committee and its activities in the consciousness of the community.

This latter objective was also served by a preliminary report which was circulated "semiprivately" among the faculty late in the spring of 1965. As one member put it, this report "drew blood" primarily because it insisted that the entire university shared the responsibility for whatever weaknesses there might be in undergraduate education.

*Education at Berkeley* is unique among the reports reviewed in this study because it included a substantial minority report. It was written by Prof. George C. Pimental. From the beginning, apparently, communication between Professor Pimental and other members of the committee was difficult. His minority report was unexpectedly introduced to the committee at the very last minute, before the final printing of the report. The rest of the committee had made continued efforts to accommodate his views, and several members stated that the committee report would have gone much further in some areas ∮f Professor Pimental's decision to issue a minority report had been announced earlier in the committee's deliberations.

Beyond the specific minority report, the committee's processes appear to have involved a good deal of compromising of rather different views. One member stated, "I asked for only about 25 percent of what I really wanted," though this must be put in the context of another member's comment that "Each of us had many of his cherished proposals deflated by the rest of the committee." Some compromise was undoubtedly inevitable in a committee consciously selected to include a spectrum of viewpoints. In addition, Professor Muscatine, especially, appears to have been anxious to produce "a report which the faculty could accept." Several members referred to this objective, though there is no indication that it was a conscious policy. For example, one committee member suggested to me that the committee retreated considerably from its already agreed-upon position on matters such as grading and examinations as a result of the reception given to one of its staff reports. Another member strongly disagreed with this view.

The committee produced its report about 11 months after it began its work. Chancellor Meyerson stated that he had originally hoped for a report within a very much shorter time in order to take advantage of the crisis situation. However, given the scope of the Muscatine study, the fact that committee members were not able to give full time to it, and the majority-minority nature of much of its deliberations, getting the report out in 11 months is a tribute to Professor Muscatine's leadership and to the dedication of the committee members.

**SUMMARY OF THE RECOM-MENDATIONS**

*Education at Berkeley* included 42 recommendations for action by the Academic Senate. Many of these were in the nature of general policy recommendations calling upon the administration, the colleges, or the departments to develop specific implementation. Some of the recommendations were rather specifically related to local issues; those of more general import are briefly summarized below.

**Educational Innovation**

The key recommendations of the committee called for some new institutional arrangements which would facilitate and encourage educational innovation and experimentation. Not only were these key in terms of the interest aroused at Berkeley and elsewhere, but members of the committee saw them in this light, too. One member suggested that these various arrangements reflected the concern of the committee with the problem of "After us, what?" The committee intended—with these recommendations—to create a formal institutional center for continuing educational change.

Specifically, the committee called for a Board of Educational Development, a vice-chancellor for educational development, and a Council for Special Curricula. The board would be empowered to approve, for up to five years, proposals for courses and programs "for which neither departmental nor college support is appropriate or feasible." It was expected that many of these proposals would be initiated by students, though faculty sponsorship was required. The council, which was the Board of Educational Development and the regular Educational Policy Committee of the Academic Senate, would be authorized to serve as sponsor for B.A. or B.S. degrees in situations where "an experimental program of courses acceptable in intellectual content or quality [exists] but no college or school is ready to accept it" or when a specific program is approved and delegated by the Academic Senate. The new vice-chancellor would be responsible for administering the activities of the B.E.D. and, in general, for encouraging and releasing financial support for experimental programs, though in spite of the urging of some committee members, a separate budget for the B.E.D. was not proposed.

Closely allied to these structural changes were proposals for ready offering of ad hoc courses on topics outside the departmental framework which might be originated by faculty or students, for interdisciplinary university courses, and for an experimental program of freshman seminars. Also proposed was a limited amount of supervised field study for academic credit. The committee suggested that field study might be undertaken on a full-time basis during some academic time period or carried on as part-time work off the campus along with regular courses.

**Teaching**  The committee devoted an entire chapter of its report to the improvement of teaching. It recognized that "the campus as a whole has not yet achieved that atmosphere or ethos of devotion to teaching that it must have in order to maintain its scholarly excellence." The committee made recommendations designed to ensure that teaching would be considered more fully in every appointment to tenure rank. The key element in its proposals was provision for a full dossier on teaching performance—including course materials, a statement by the candidate on his teaching, and written evaluations of the candidate's performance based on classroom visitations by colleagues.

Also recommended were steps to ensure a greater number of small discussion classes and greater faculty participation in lower-division teaching. An experimental program of student course evaluation was also called for.

Because Berkeley relied heavily on teaching assistants, many of the report's recommendations in this regard are relevant to the overall question of teaching. Basically, these called for much more emphasis on teaching in the selection and training of teaching assistants, whom the study had found were too often treated without professional respect by faculty members. It was also proposed to improve the stipends of teaching assistants and to make them more competitive with many research assistantships and fellowships. (As has been true nationally, many of the best graduate students at Berkeley did not take teaching assistantships.)

**Advising**  The report included a discussion of academic advising and orientation and concluded that the system—at least in the 12,000-student College of Letters and Science—was woefully inadequate. The committee discussed a number of possible improvements: mechanization of student recordkeeping, a continuation of a recently inaugurated summer orientation program, better information, employment of faculty specialists in advising, and freshman courses which would place an emphasis on the advising as well as the teaching role of the faculty member. Beyond these, the committee simply recommended that the advising system be made entirely voluntary, on the grounds that no system at all was better than a positively harmful one.

**Grading**  The Muscatine Committee commissioned a special study on grading. The report on this study—the Miller report—was issued to the faculty while the Muscatine study was still in process. It met with a less than friendly reception, and so the Muscatine Committee included in its report a number of somewhat modified recommendations. These included provision for the student election of one course in each term (excluding courses in the student's major) on a pass-fail basis. Also, faculty members would be allowed to offer one course each term on a pass-fail basis with only departmental approval. It was also recommended that the courses taken during the student's first term in residence be excluded from calculation of the grade-point average.

**Curriculum**  Most of the committee's discussion of general curriculum changes concerned the College of Letters and Science, which is where most of the students and most of the problems seemed to be. It did propose that the professional schools and colleges join with the College of Letters and Science in the development of combined five-year, B.A.-B.S. programs and that the College of Letters and Science offer "more effective general courses and programs in humanities and Social Sciences" so that the professional schools would be in a position to raise their breadth requirements to 20 to 25 percent of the total degree requirements. In the College of Letters and Science there had been, since 1957, a breadth or distribution requirement which involved English reading and composition, a foreign language, and courses in three traditional areas. Compared with those of many institutions, the Berkeley requirement was rather loose in that, except for English and foreign languages, the requirement could be met at any time during the student's four years and could be satisfied by a wide range of introductory and advanced courses. The principal change proposed by the report was that the distribution requirements be separated into "inner-breadth" and "outer-breadth" courses. The former would be courses outside, but related to, the student's major field. Outer-breadth courses would involve areas quite removed from the student's major area of interest. The outer-breadth distribution would be required, while selection of inner-breadth courses would be left largely to the student and his adviser.

**Graduate Education**

Several recommendations were made which aimed at broadening and debureaucratizing graduate programs. These would encourage programs more directly related to the student's own interests, more flexibility in language requirements, more interdisciplinary programs, and granting credit for work relating the graduate curriculum to problems of teaching. Perhaps the key proposal was one for the creation of a doctor of arts degree which would be awarded after completion of the usual Ph.D. course work but without completion of a dissertation. The obvious intent was to provide a program for those who would teach, but not be professional researchers.

**Student Participation**

The committee argued against student membership on regular faculty committees, but urged that "faculty and administration should regularly consult students' views on educational policy." Development of permanent arrangements for a liaison between campus-wide faculty and student committees was called for.

**OVERALL IMPACT OF THE RECOMMENDATIONS**

On the whole, the Muscatine recommendations represented an attempt to minimize the bureaucratic character of a large, heterogeneous campus and to bring the undergraduate student back from the very periphery of the educational activity of the university. Improvement of teaching and greater freedom and flexibility for students were the principal directions chosen for achieving these ends. The Board of Educational Development and related proposals were central in the report. As an institutional arrangement, the board would surely provide an opportunity for innovation and change. The provision of formal trial periods for new developments made possible the permanent adoption of proved alternatives for existing courses, programs, and processes. On the other hand, such an arrangement—separated from "regular" educational activities —could also isolate innovation and change from much of the campus. That is, it would provide freedom for those who wished to innovate, but would permit those who preferred to go on in the old way to do just that, secure in the knowledge that Berkeley was responding to demands for "reform" and "relevance." And the proposal for much more stringent evaluation of teaching in tenure decisions is crucial here. For unless the innovative, student-centered teaching activities which the proposal for the board contemplates are to be rewarded and not penalized, it is not very profound to suggest that such activities would be limited. That is, if promotion and the rest continue to be made on the same departmental basis with the traditional criteria applying, few are likely to risk much time or effort on innovation and change in teaching—even under the aegis of the board.

**CONSIDERA-
TION OF
THE REPORT**

The committee's report was issued on March 22, 1966—just a year after the adoption of the resolution which created the committee. Officially the report was addressed to the Academic Senate, and its disposition was in the hands of the leaders of that body. In fact, Professor Muscatine and some other committee members were very much involved in steering the report through the Academic Senate. Professor Muscatine made the crucial decision about the order in which recommendations would be brought up for consideration and acted as one of the floor leaders during most of the debates. More than one person referred to his performance during this period as "brilliant," and one committee member said that he "worked himself to death." Professor Muscatine suggested that Berkeley had a "highly articulated legislative system" and that it was important that he and several other committee members knew well the workings of the system as they prepared for the consideration of a complex series of proposals.

The key decision was to introduce first into the Academic Senate the recommendations concerning the Board of Educational Development and related matters. The committee regarded these as the key, and most controversial, recommendations in their report and, in effect, presented them as the basis for a vote of confidence. There was a sense that the momentum that arose from the trauma of the Free Speech Movement and was sustained through the committee's study and the report would be sufficient to carry through these proposals. And such was the case. The debates on these proposals went on through two Academic Senate meetings with about 1,000 faculty members present. Professor Pimental's minority position was thoroughly aired in these meetings, but with only minor changes the Board of

Educational Development, the Council for Special Curricula, and the assistant chancellor for educational development[2] were approved by the senate in the spring of 1966.

The pass-fail options for students and faculty were also passed in the spring. In some ways the committee's proposals were made more restrictive, but they were also liberalized by the acceptance of "pass–not pass" terminology, which means, at Berkeley, that the "not pass" does not affect the student's average. At the same time, the proposal to leave the student's first-quarter grades out of his average was defeated. Also during the spring, certain steps to involve students in university government were passed. These actions went somewhat beyond the committee's proposals by providing for student membership on certain committees and participation by the president of the Associated Students (without vote) in the Academic Senate.

The trade edition of *Education at Berkeley,* published in 1968, contains a summary of the action taken on each of the specific recommendations which need not be repeated here. It is quite clear from this record that the momentum which carried several recommendations through in the spring had largely dissipated by the fall. As one committee member put it, "By then the heat was off." The rather revolutionary proposals for strengthening the evaluation of teaching were largely ignored in a much-watered-down resolution which was eventually passed. Several recommendations were referred to other committees, and the formal consideration of the report essentially ended in February, 1967, when a number of proposals which had not been previously acted upon were "received and placed on file" by the Academic Senate. In addition, the several recommendations affecting the College of Letters and Science specifically had to be reconsidered by that faculty, and many of them disappeared in that process. It must also be recognized that many of the matters left until fall were matters which were much less susceptible to formal legislative action.

**OVERALL RESULTS** In terms of its specific recommendations, the Berkeley committee achieved its greatest success in gaining acceptance for the Board of Educational Development and proposals related to it. The

---

[2] This was a change of some substance, since the original proposal called for a vice-chancellor who, under the California organization, would report to the chancellor. The assistant chancellor reported to the vice-chancellor for Academic affairs.

decision to embark on the study was made at a time of deep crisis. Whether out of fear or guilt (and both have been suggested by various Berkeley faculty members) a slim majority of the Academic Senate was ready to pick up Chancellor Meyerson's suggestion for a study of education at Berkeley. By holding open hearings, issuing interim reports, and conducting a fair amount of interview-based research, the committee kept itself and its activity rather at stage front. When the report came out, it received considerable attention in the national press, and in a sense all eyes were still on Berkeley. The committee capitalized on this by pushing its most controversial and perhaps most fundamental proposals—those relating to the Board of Educational Development—immediately to the front.

Beyond this, the committee did succeed in bringing about elimination of some of the rigidities which had come to surround education in the university and in focusing some needed attention on the undergraduates. Whether more sweeping changes would have been made had the majority-minority situation not developed in the committee must, of course, remain unknown. Certainly the committee would have made proposals which were more challenging to the Berkeley faculty. An indication that the faculty moved about as far as could be expected at that time is found in comments made to me by several committee members who observed that the study had restored the respectability of discussing educational problems at Berkeley. Given that a sizable minority of the Academic Senate voted against establishment of the committee, this is an achievement of consequence. On the other hand, an environment in which discussion of educational matters is out of the ordinary is not likely to be one in which much real educational change will occur. It must also give one pause to think that it would be necessary, in an educational institution, to restore respectability to discussion of educational probems.

# 3. University of
# New Hampshire

## Toward Unity from Diversity

The University of New Hampshire began as the state "A. & M. college," but after broadening its curricula to include the arts and sciences in the early years of this century, it came to have many of the characteristics associated with small New England colleges. In recent years, however, explosive growth in enrollments and expansion of graduate programs have changed that character. In 1967, the university enrolled about 6,100 full-time students, including nearly 800 graduate students, and had a faculty of some 400. Ten years earlier, the student body had numbered under 3,500, and the faculty under 200. New Hampshire is unusual among state universities in that over one-quarter of its student body comes from outside the state.

In 1967, the university had no graduate professional schools, but the Ph.D. was awarded in 10 fields, and master's work was offered in many departments. In addition to the traditional majors in the arts and sciences, the university had undergraduate professional programs in a number of occupational specialties. Academic programs were centered in the graduate school and four undergraduate colleges—liberal arts, agriculture (which included certain basic science departments), technology (which included physics, mathematics, and chemistry as well as the engineering departments), and the Whittemore School of Business and Economics. Each of these units was headed by a dean, and each college or school had a great deal of power. As one dean stated it, "This University has been and continues to be 'college-centered.'"

In 1967, the focus for university-wide policy making and governance was centered in the University Senate, which included an elected representative from each department, along with other elected and *ex officio* members. The seven-man Faculty Council, representing the colleges and chosen from among senate members, served as an executive committee and met regularly with the president. It nominated members for standing committees of the senate and the faculty members on other committees of the administration.

In late November of 1965, primarily at the urging of one of the college deans, an ad hoc university-wide Educational Policies Committee was established. It was charged with making a comprehensive study of the educational policies of the university and began its work in December, 1965. In October, 1966, it issued a preliminary draft report. During October, members of the university considered and reacted to this draft report in formal and informal group meetings. The ad hoc committee reviewed its report during November and December, 1966, and its final report was issued in February, 1967.

During the spring of 1967, a number of informal meetings were held to discuss the report, but no formal consideration was given to any recommendations by the University Senate until the fall of 1967. The senate and the university administration considered proposals from the committee during most of the 1967–68 academic year. By February, 1969, with perhaps two-thirds of the proposals having been acted upon in one way or another, active consideration of the report had apparently ceased.

**ORIGIN OF THE STUDY** The idea of a wide-ranging study of New Hampshire's educational policies was suggested to the academic deans and senior university administrators by Dean Robert F. Barlow of the Whittemore school. In his formal proposal, he referred to:

[1] . . . the evident unrest and dissatisfaction with the quality of education we are now providing among the more intelligent and serious members of the undergraduate student body, and (2) apparent dissatisfaction on this point among members of the faculty who are deeply concerned not only with the current status of our undergraduate education but with its future development. A number of faculty members have mentioned this matter to me and several have expressed frustration about their inability to do anything about it.

The deans were generally enthusiastic about the idea of a major study. Some consideration was given to having the study done by one of the regular standing committees of the University Senate, but there was a general feeling that neither the usual membership nor the normal operating stance of the standing committees would be appropriate for such a sweeping study, and eventually the idea of a special committee was agreed upon.

President John W. McConnell took the proposal to the Faculty Council. This group debated such issues as the scope of the committee's inquiry, released time and budgetary support for committee members, selection of the committee, and to whom the latter should finally report. As the following resolution passed by the Faculty Council indicates, most of the issues were left undecided in any formal way:

That the Chairman of the Faculty Council be directed to request the President to initiate, at an early date a comprehensive study of the educational policies of the University of New Hampshire and to present on or before February 1, 1967, through the Faculty Council to the Senate of the University and the Faculty such proposals for strengthening and improvement of those educational policies as result from such study. Occasional progress reports to the Faculty Council would be welcome.

The creation of the committee and the makeup of its membership were subsequently announced to the University Senate, but no vote by the senate was asked for or proposed, and there was very little discussion of the announcement.

Essentially, then, the decision to undertake the study at New Hampshire was an administrative one and, on the whole, was seen that way by most of the faculty. The dissatisfactions referred to in the original proposal to establish the committee were no doubt present, but there is no indication of any widespread demand for such a study on the part of either faculty or students. Indeed, only five years earlier the university had had a similar though more narrowly focused review, and at least some faculty members wondered why another study was needed. Generally speaking, the announcement of the study was greeted without particular hostility or notable enthusiasm.

SELECTION OF THE COMMITTEE It is normal practice at New Hampshire for each of the colleges to have more or less pro rata representation on all university committees, and no thought was given to a departure from this tradition in forming the University-wide Educational Policies Committee. Each of the deans was asked to nominate members from his faculty. The deans and the president had agreed that neither seniority nor the established position of potential members should be considered. Indeed, as the data on committee membership suggest, there was a bias against people who had been associated with the university for a long time. President McConnell has stated that he was interested in people who were concerned with education generally and especially those who were interested in new approaches to education. Faculty members who were articulate and who had provided leadership were also sought after. No particular thought was given to the probability of the members' being able to work together. Indeed, several members of the committee had never met until its first meeting. Nor was any thought given to the inclusion of either students or persons from outside the university. Having members of the administration on the committee was not considered, although two members were department chairmen. Final selection of the committee and designation of the chairman were made by the president and Dean Barlow. The chairman-designate was asked to take on the assignment in an interview with the president. Other members were asked to serve in a letter from the president.

Announcement of committee membership was received by most of the faculty without public excitement. Most of the committee members were not well known outside their respective colleges, and with perhaps one exception none of those who were known were especially controversial figures. There was rather more consternation expressed privately. Some were drawn to the conclusion

**TABLE 2** *Membership of the University-wide Educational Policies Committee, University of New Hampshire (UNH)*

| Name and rank | Field | Age group* | Years at UNH | Degrees from UNH |
|---|---|---|---|---|
| Richard Balomenos, assistant professor | Mathematics | 34–41 | 4 | None |
| Robert Corell, associate professor | Mechanical engineering | Under 33 | 1 | None |
| Raymond Erickson, associate professor | Psychology | 34–41 | 2 | None |
| Herman Gadon, associate professor | Business administration | 42–49 | 1 | None |
| Francis Hall, associate professor | Soil and water science | 34–41 | 1 | None |
| Hans Heilbronner, professor | History | 34–41 | 11 | None |
| Dwight Ladd, professor | Business administration | 42–49 | 1 | None |
| Asher Moore, professor | Philosophy | 42–49 | 4 | None |
| Donald Murray, associate professor | English | 34–41 | 2 | B.A. |
| Richard Strout, associate professor | Animal science | 34–41 | 11 | M.S., Ph.D. |

*Ages and years at the institution are given as of the time the committee was first convened.

that the lack of seniority of most committee members meant that they would be "tools of the administration." More significantly, many faculty members—especially those strongly imbued with the liberal arts tradition—were concerned about the number of committee members who came from "applied" fields. One critic of the committee wrote, "Among the undoubtedly able young men tapped to serve appeared none who might be suspected of harboring educational values akin to those of Jacques Barzun or even Robert Hutchins." None of the fears of these people was quieted by selection of a recently appointed professor of business administration as chairman of the committee.

**CONDUCT OF THE STUDY** The committee's terms of reference were extremely broad, but in an initial meeting with President McConnell it was agreed that the primary focus of the study should be on undergraduate education. The committee was also told that it need not be concerned with the costs of its recommendations nor with the problems of implementation. The committee itself agreed to begin its work by attempting to compile an inventory of policy problems rather than by attempting to develop a framework of educational philosophy.

In the first phase of its work, the committee sent a letter to all faculty members asking them to communicate to the committee any educational policy issues which were of concern to them. The same invitation was conveyed to students through the student newspaper. Some 50 replies were received from faculty members, and none from students. During the early weeks of its work, the committee interviewed most of the deans and senior administrative officials. The question of bringing in outside consultants was raised within the committee on numerous occasions, but a decision to do so was always deferred until the committee agreed that some particular advice was needed. That point never came.

The committee regularly had two long meetings each week and several all-day meetings during vacation periods. In addition, the committee had several weekend meetings away from the campus. On the whole, the committee conducted its business as a unit, although different individuals or groups prepared position papers on various topics. Generally speaking, the committee appears to have been an effective working group.

In the late spring, the committee concluded that it could produce a preliminary draft of its report by early fall. They felt that maximum possible involvement in its work by all members of the university was desirable and could be achieved through widespread discussion of such a preliminary draft. The idea was raised by the chairman in a meeting with the president and the Faculty Council, and a decision was made to go ahead.

Consideration of the preliminary draft was to be done by a number of study groups including faculty, students, administrators, and members of the Board of Trustees. Each department designated a member to participate in one of the study groups, and the officers of the student government designated student members. After some discussion, the student government leaders urged that students join in separate study groups rather than be mixed in with faculty, administrators, and trustees. They felt that students would be inhibited from an open expression of their views.[1] Ultimately, nine study groups were formed: three with student members and six with faculty, administrators, and some trustees included. One member of the committee sat on each study group.

Mimeographed copies of the preliminary report were distributed to all faculty members, and the entire report was made available to all students through a special supplement to the student newspaper. Most of the study groups met about twice a week during the month of October. Each study group decided whether to make some written report to the committee or to rely upon the committee member sitting with them to carry their views to the committee. Most groups chose the latter method. In addition to meeting with the study groups, the entire committee appeared at an open hearing sponsored by the New Hampshire chapter of the American Association of University Professors (AAUP). There was a sizable faculty turnout at this meeting. During this period many departments chose to hold meetings to discuss the draft report, and several of these submitted statements to the committee. In October the draft report was the principal topic of concern and conversation among the faculty. Except among those who were members of the study groups there was very little student involvement. Some of the student study-group members attempted to organize dormitory meetings and the like, but generally these were unsuccessful.

[1] It is startling to recall that this decision was made by students in 1966. Two short years later students were demanding equal representation on all faculty committees and governing bodies. It is difficult to think of present student leaders as being in any way inhibited by their elders. The 1966 view is clearly a reflection of the inherent conservatism of most New Hampshire students, but also indicated by this situation is the tremendous speed with which the student power movement has taken hold.

Reaction to the preliminary report was mixed. President McConnell publicly indicated his general support of its conclusions and proposals on several occasions, and many faculty members—especially the younger ones—indicated their enthusiasm. Opposition centered around two of the committee's proposals: (1) substitution of the course for the credit hour as the basis for academic bookkeeping and a reduction in the number of courses required for graduation and (2) a substantial opening up of the university general education requirements. In the case of the first issue, most of the opposition came from within departments with professional or applied work whose curricula were characterized by many one- and two-credit courses and from within departments whose rather rigidly sequential curricula were thought to require more courses. Opposition to the second proposal centered among some of the humanists and social scientists. They were concerned that students would no longer be required to study those things "which every educated man should know" and that students could satisfy general education requirements in, for example, creative writing or business. In addition, there were many among those more extensively concerned with graduate work who felt that the report, in its emphasis and in some of its phraseology, tended to downgrade graduate work.

At the end of October, the committee retired to prepare its final report. A number of changes in emphasis and detail were made in light of the reactions to the preliminary report, but there were no changes in the basic, overall direction of the recommendations. The final report was issued on February 15, 1967. All faculty members received copies, and the entire report was printed as a supplement to the student newspaper.

**SUMMARY OF THE RECOM- MENDATIONS** The report included some 75 recommendations which were identified as requiring faculty action, administrative action, or joint action. The important recommendations which are not exclusively concerned with local issues are summarized below.

**Curriculum** The committee proposed substitution of the course for the credit hour as the basis for academic bookkeeping and recommended that four courses per semester be the normal student load, with five as a maximum. Thirty-two courses, rather than 128 credit hours, would be the minimum required for graduation.

The number of courses which could be required for a major would be limited to 16 (one-half the student's load), and college requirements would be eliminated. Thus the student would meet only university requirements (see below) and requirements for the major. The balance of his program would be freely elected. (Most of the colleges had some curricular requirements. The proposed limitation on the major would affect mainly the sciences and the several professional programs.)

All New Hampshire students, regardless of college or field, had been required to meet a university general education requirement. This included freshman English, contemporary civilization, and one year's work in each of the following: the natural sciences, the social sciences, and the humanities. These latter courses were chosen by the student from a fairly restricted list of departmental courses—mostly at the introductory level. The committee recommended replacing all these requirements with four semester courses in the sciences (including mathematics) and six semester courses from among the social sciences, the humanities, and the arts. Any course—introductory or advanced—would satisfy these requirements, and all departments were urged to eliminate as many as possible of their prerequisites for advanced courses. (There was no university language requirement, but the committee proposed that the language requirement for the B.A. degree be made a departmental requirement as an interim step and ultimately become an admission requirement for all students.)

A pass-fail option for eight courses outside the major was recommended by the committee with the further proposal that after a three-year trial period, all courses except those for the major be pass-fail.

**Curriculum Administration**

In order to provide for more university-wide attention to general education, the committee recommended appointment of a dean for general education. It was suggested that such a dean could "maintain a continuing review of the undergraduate general education activites of the university. Working with and through the departments and college deans, he could facilitate the development of new general education programs, some of which might cross departmental and college boundaries." This dean would provide a locus for conducting experiments in general education and would be "basically concerned with innovation . . . and the continuing development of general education programs."

The committee also proposed the creation of a broadly based

undergraduate council to support a commitment "to the equality of general education with other university activities." This council would have the authority to approve general-education courses and programs—especially those which crossed college and departmental boundaries.

**Teaching and Advising**　The report discussed the question of quality of teaching at some length and proposed more positive attention to teaching in decisions about salary and promotion. Development of procedures for evaluation of teaching by all concerned—including students—was proposed.

The committee also recommended a program of seminars for all freshmen and asked that each department develop ways of teaching in small sections some of the courses usually taken to meet general education requirements. The committee urged that other courses be taught in relatively large groups, arguing that a mixture of quite small and quite large classes would better serve the student than the rather widespread format of middle-sized classes.

The committee also urged the departments to offer courses which were not conceived of as steps in a progression for the major or for graduate school admission. A special review of the potential effect on undergraduate programs of any proposed new graduate program was also proposed.

The study included a discussion of academic advising which argued that effective advising on academic matters could be done only in the context of the student-teacher relationship. This conclusion was a major reason behind the recommendation for freshman seminars. Essentially, however, the committee's recommendations dealt with housekeeping matters.

**Climate of the University**　The committee was concerned with the rigid compartmentalization of "academics" away from all other aspects of university life and proposed that faculty members should be associated with student residences in a variety of ways, including locating faculty offices in dormitories and having in-resident faculty fellows. Incorporation of some teaching in the residences was also proposed. A further recommendation was that with the association of academic with residential activities, the residential groups could make any rules necessary for their own comfort and convenience and that the university, as such, should abolish all rules concerned with student conduct and living. In addition it was recommended that the dean of students and his associates be made a part of the office of the academic vice-president on the grounds that "every aspect of what a student does while here is an academic affair."

**Other Matters** In addition to suggesting a number of changes in the internal structure of the university, the committee proposed that its rapid growth be checked. (On a relative basis, the University of New Hampshire is not large, but the committee argued that the university was large enough because of its limited financial resources, its rural location, and the importance of permitting "most students and most faculty to have some identification—other than through a winning football team—with the totality of the institution.")

**OVERALL IMPACT OF THE PROPOSALS** The report of the New Hampshire committee proposed some fairly sweeping changes for the university. The change in the academic accounting system and the reduction in the number of courses to be taken would, if seriously implemented, require a rather thorough rethinking of the whole curriculum. A number of the proposals were intended to create a counterbalance within the university to the power of the departments in matters of educational policy generally and to bring about an atmosphere in which innovation and experimentation would be more generally encouraged.

The proposals concerning residences and related matters would, if adopted, tend to lead to an atmosphere and structure more nearly approaching the idea of "community." While the specific curriculum changes were not especially far-reaching in terms of what the university was doing, the proposals for freshman seminars, more small classes, and reductions in course loads would require fundamental changes in the basic educational processes of the university.

**CONSIDERATION OF THE REPORT** While the final report was being prepared, members of the committee and senior administrators discussed how consideration of the report would be handled. Members of the committee felt that they should not be actively involved in these processes. The academic vice-president was ultimately given overall responsibility for carrying out consideration of the recommendations, and he appointed a five-man steering committee to advise him. This committee met once and arranged the report's recommendations in a logical order for discussion in planned open meetings of the University Senate. Three such meetings, chaired by the president, were held over a two-month period during the spring. During this same period, the president met once with each of the study groups which had been formed to consider the preliminary report. Both of these series of meetings were intended to provide for a broad expression of reactions to the report's recommendations.

By the end of the spring semester, none of the proposals requiring faculty action had been brought before the senate, nor had any obvious action been taken by the administration on proposals directed to it. Consequently, at the last meeting of the senate in the spring, a member asked what was being done with the report. In the absence of any plan for consideration, a motion made from the floor to send the report to the Curricula Committee of the senate was passed.

In the fall of 1967, the Curricula Committee began to introduce resolutions for implementing the ad hoc committee's recommendations. Most of these followed quite closely the proposals of the report; some were modified to take into account known objections. Because the Curricula Committee was concerned with specific rules, the formal discussions of the report did not begin with any consideration of the general policy commitments which the report had proposed and which underlay most of its recommendations. Rather, the senate immediately became involved with specific proposals, each of which directly affected some special interest. Furthermore, these specific proposals required, under the senate bylaws, a three-quarter majority for passage. Discussion was, in general, desultory and often rancorous. For example, four meetings of roughly two hours each were required to dispose of the committee's recommendation that required physical education be eliminated. The proposal to shift from 128 credit hours to 32 courses for graduation and a normal four-course per semester student program became entangled with the question of the academic calendar. (Three 3-course terms were proposed as an alternative.) Discussion was suspended for several weeks while a special committee investigated calendar alternatives. Eventually, the semester system was retained, but a reading period between the end of classes and the examination period was incorporated into each semester. The four-course proposal was implemented by having the normal course carry four credits. The substance of the committee's recommendations for general-education requirements was adopted, though the proposal to eliminate college requirements was rejected, and the recommended limitation on major requirements lessened. The pass-fail option was approved for four courses outside the major rather than the eight proposed. Most of the academic year 1967–68 was consumed in deliberations on these matters, and by the fall of 1968, the incentive to consider any more of the committee's proposals appeared to be pretty well gone.

During the period of senate discussion of matters relating to curriculum, there was little overt action on other proposals in the report. The university administration did discuss most of these other proposals and made a number of decisions regarding them, but the decisions were not generally publicized. Plans for a new dormitory-dining complex were revised to incorporate facilities for faculty in residence, but no action was taken to implement any of the alternative suggestions for existing dormitories. The several recommendations relating to the administration of the undergraduate curriculum and general education were referred to an administration committee which, by the summer of 1969, had not reported. Various proposals for emphasizing quality of teaching were considered within the administration, but only limited action has followed. The proposal for limiting enrollment was rejected — at least for the time being. Certain of the proposals for internal administrative structure — expanding the central administration, for example — were implemented. Others were still in the hands of committees in the spring of 1969. The proposal to bring the dean of students under the academic vice-president was rejected.

**OVERALL RESULTS** Except in certain areas relating to curriculum, the specific recommendations of the New Hampshire report had limited impact. The change to a four-course system may have important effects on the curriculum after it goes into effect in the fall of 1969. Student choices of courses have been made somewhat freer. Except for the dormitory complex under construction, there has been no effect on the basic nature of the residences. Partly as a result of the study and partly as a result of subsequent events, the structure of university government has been revised.[2]

It is also the case that many of the structural and environmental

---

[2] In the spring of 1969, the university adopted a unicameral system of government. The old University Senate and a Student Senate were replaced by a University Senate consisting of 30 elected faculty members, 30 elected undergraduates, 5 elected graduate students, and 12 *ex officio* administrators. This University Senate will have all the powers exercised by the two senates which it replaced. De jure, at any rate, New Hampshire students do have the equal voice so widely demanded.

changes designed to permit more experimentation and innovation through greater flexibility and leadership have not been implemented. The powers of the departments and colleges which the report sought to diminish—however obliquely—remain as strong as ever. The attempt of the committee to move toward a rather more unified institution in which general education would be at least as important as specialization and in which faculty, students, and administration would be more consciously involved in a common and broad educational experience was not successful.

On the other hand, there are some at New Hampshire who feel that the overall process of the study had an effect beyond the actions taken or not taken with respect to particular proposals. Specifically, they feel that the study did have the effect of somewhat "opening up" the institution. The relatively ready acceptance of the change in university government, or the inauguration, in 1969, of an experimental, nondepartmental program for freshman and sophomores, for example, would not have been possible, in the opinion of some, without the preceding discussions of the policy study. In short, some feel that the study helped to create an atmosphere in which change and innovation can be more readily considered and accepted.

# 4. University of Toronto

## Undergraduate Instruction in Arts and Sciences

In terms of both structure and style, the University of Toronto combines many elements of Oxbridge and the Scottish universities, the Ivy League institutions, and the Big Ten. It is academically the most prestigious Canadian university. It has a great deal of social prestige and yet functions as a streetcar college. Some of its constituent elements are privately endowed, while others are heavily supported by the Province of Ontario. It includes several church-sponsored colleges and universities and yet is the official provincial university. In addition to its Faculty of Arts and Sciences, the university has 17 professional faculties and schools, which in 1968–69 enrolled about 24,000 full-time students and 7,200 part-time students.

In part, Toronto is a federation of independent colleges and universities: Victoria University (United Church), University of Trinity College (Anglican), and University of St. Michael's College (Roman Catholic), in addition to a number of theological colleges. University College is nonsectarian and is part of the constituent university. These four are the "old colleges," which joined—along with several professional schools—to form the University of Toronto between 1887 and 1903. In recent years, four new colleges have been created. Two of these are located on the main Toronto campus, and each of the other two has its own campus about 20 miles away. The federated universities and colleges are partly administrative units, partly residential and social organizations, and partly academic entities. Each of the four old federated universities teaches classics, English, French, German, and Near Eastern studies, and those which are church-sponsored universities also teach ethics and religious knowledge. St. Michael's teaches philosophy as well. The federated universities teach these subjects in the fullest sense of the word. Each has its own budgets and departments and makes its own faculty appointments. In addition, Toronto has a graduate department and a combined undergraduate department in each of these subjects, made up wholly of the members of the college departments. Instruction in areas other than those mentioned is given by university departments. Ultimately, the Faculty of Arts and Science of the university is the degree-granting body, and all members of the federated departments are members of that faculty. That this organization is cumbersome and overlapping is generally understood at Toronto, but it has survived several attempts at restructuring, for the traditions behind the old colleges and their political power are not inconsequential.

One other characteristic of the University of Toronto needs explanation for those not familiar with the Canadian educational system. The undergraduate in the University of Toronto takes either a general course or an honours course. The general course (often referred to as "pass arts") involves three years in the university after the five-year Ontario High School. Honours courses require four years after grade 13. The general course is rather a grab bag of subjects, though in recent years the American concept of the major has become more and more accepted and used. The honours courses involve highly structured, intensive, and specialized study in a single field or combination of fields. In general, it is probably correct that the graduate of an honours course has roughly the equivalent of an American M.A.

For the most part, students in general programs and honours programs are rather thoroughly segregated. Lower admissions and graduation standards are in effect for general-course students. While honours students typically receive a great deal of care and feeding from the faculty, the general-course students have, to a considerable degree, been left to fend for themselves. The honours programs have long been the "jewels in Toronto's crown," and their widely recognized excellence is a matter of fierce pride for most faculty members and graduates. In recent times, as enrollment increased, there has been a marked trend away from honours and toward the general course. In 1961, 39 percent of the entering class was enrolled in the general program. By 1966, the percentage had increased to 47.

The Presidential Advisory Committee on Undergraduate Instruction in the Faculty of Arts and Sciences was appointed by President Bissell in the spring of 1966. The committee issued its report in late July, 1967, though it was October, 1967 before the report was printed and distributed to the faculty generally. At the time the report was distributed, the chairman of the committee and the president were both on leave from the university, and little formal action was taken at the overall faculty level, although extensive discussion did begin within departments and colleges. During the latter part of the 1967–68 academic year, the dean of the Faculty of Arts and Sciences took the report under advisement with an ad hoc committee. During the summer of 1968, this group issued an interim report recommending to the faculty a number of immediate actions. By the time this report came before the council (which is, in effect, the entire teaching faculty plus 16 elected students[1]) in September, 1968, the student power movement had arrived in Toronto, and membership of students on important committees was accepted. As a result, a new committee including one staff member and one student from each department was created to advise the dean. Because the Faculty of Arts and Sciences includes 25 departments, it became known as the "Committee of Fifty."

During the fall and winter of 1968–69 this committee, under Dean A. D. Allen, brought to the council a proposal for a new undergraduate program. This new program was based on the recommendations of the original presidential committee but involved a number of modifications in detail and in basic philosophy. It was accepted by the council on February 20, 1969.

Parts of the original report that concerned restructuring and the general environment of the university had not been considered in any regular, formal way by late spring of 1969.

**ORIGIN OF THE STUDY**   The decision to undertake a wide-ranging study of undergraduate education at Toronto was made essentially by President Claude Bissell. He said that several factors brought him to a consideration of such a step. For one thing, he believed that "left-wing pressures" in Canada would, in the absence of such issues as Vietnam and civil rights, focus on the educational process, and he wished to head this off as much as possible. Also, Toronto had been expanding graduate work rapidly, and he was concerned about maintaining a balance between that and undergraduate studies. He was also concerned about the increasingly large number of very large classes in the university and about the

---

[1] These students were first added to council membership in the spring of 1968.

heavy reliance on lectures and examinations in the teaching process. He stated that he had received many reports of increasingly poor quality of teaching.

Other members of the university suggested other factors in the decision to undertake the study: the continuing problem of the federated colleges, wide criticism of the second-class nature of the general course, and the overspecialization of the honours program. One administrator suggested that the study also represented a "pious attempt" to compensate for the lack of money and facilities required to meet the problems of size.

Virtually everyone at Toronto appears to have been much concerned about one or more of these problems, but there is also no indication that there was any organized focus for this concern, no widely shared thought that such a study should be embarked upon. The idea of undertaking it appears to have been President Bissell's alone. When the study was begun, President Bissell made a commitment that any report which the committee produced would be printed and circulated. Beyond this, there was no thought about how such a report might be considered and acted upon by the university.

**SELECTION OF THE COMMITTEE** The president created the Presidential Advisory Committee, and therefore he appointed the members. It appears that Prof. C. B. Macpherson was the only person seriously considered for the chairmanship. Professor Macpherson had often served on important committees, and several persons, including the president, suggested that he was the logical choice for the job. Professor Macpherson is well known and powerful on the Toronto campus. No one referred to the study as anything but the Macpherson report, and it is obvious that most people feel that the report was largely his handiwork.

The balance of the committee was selected by the president and the chairman in consultation with others—especially the former and incumbent deans of arts and science. President Bissell suggested that they looked for relatively young people who would be receptive to innovation and who "had not been brainwashed by the honours mystique." He also wanted persons from the major disciplines and a balance among British, American, and Canadian backgrounds. The president also added an outsider—a professor from another university—primarily to offset the Toronto preoccupation with honours courses.

**TABLE 3**  *Membership of the Presidential Advisory Committee, University of Toronto*

| Name and rank | Field | Age group* | Years at Toronto | Degrees from Toronto |
|---|---|---|---|---|
| G. R. Cook, associate professor | History | 34–41 | 10 | Ph.D. |
| W. G. Friend, professor | Zoology | 34–41 | 6 | None |
| J. R. Jackson, assistant professor | English | Under 33 | 4 | None |
| C. B. Macpherson, professor | Political science | 50–57 | 33 | B.A. |
| S. C. Nyberg, professor | Chemistry | 42–49 | 4 | None |
| R. M. H. Shepherd, professor and registrar of University College | Classics | 42–49 | 19 | None |
| H. S. Harris, professor at York University (outside member) | Philosophy | | | None |
| F. H. Buck, graduate student | | | | B.A. |

*Ages and years at the institution are given as of the time the committee was first convened.

Professor Macpherson pointed out that there was no "brass" on the committee. None of the members was even a department chairman. Neither the president nor the chairman had had a close prior acquaintance with those finally chosen. Professor Macpherson inquired around the university seeking out persons who felt that changes in Toronto's educational policies were needed. A graduate student member was chosen in the same way as faculty members, though he was also designated as "research officer" so that half of his time could be paid for. One-half of the chairman's time and one-quarter of the time of the other members was "bought" by the president from the departments involved. Other than for secretarial help, the committee had no operating budget as such.

**OPERATION OF THE COMMITTEE**  While the committee was not formed as a response to any very widespread demand, it appears to have capitalized quickly on the general concern over the many issues with which it was to deal. Each faculty member, each undergraduate, and all graduates of the preceding two years were invited, by a personal letter from the committee, to make a submission to the committee. In addition, the committee held 15 public hearings. The first of these was general, and the others concerned specific issues. In addition, members of the committee dealt directly with various departments and administrators, and a detailed questionnaire dealing with many issues of class size, teaching, and the like was sent to all departments. In other words, the committee, in a variety of ways, maintained a high degree of visibility within the community from the start.

The committee appears to have done its work in a generally harmonious atmosphere. An early decision was made not to consider a philosophy of education, but rather to deal from the start with specific problems and to let recommendations develop from the analysis of these problems. All members wrote drafts and position papers on various topics, but the complete drafts were prepared by the chairman. As might be expected, members disagreed over many issues, but no permanent blocs developed within the committee. One contentious issue was the wish of some to focus more undergraduate teaching within the colleges, and the final recommendations are a tightly written compromise between the interests of university departments and collegiate teaching.

There was also considerable concern over the relationship between upgrading the general course and the possibly concomitant downgrading of the honours program. It is also clear from talking with committee members that there was uneasiness over a report on educational policy which did not concern itself with some fundamental discussion of education. Because of this uneasiness, a recommendation was made to create a new committee to study the long-range problems of the nature of general and specialist education. In spite of the recommendation, however, the principal criticism of the report that I heard from other members of the university had to do with this lack of any discussion of basic objectives. Persons may rarely agree on fundamental objectives and even less frequently act on the basis of them, but they obviously do like to read and talk about them.

Both the outside member and the student member added greatly to the committee's effectiveness. It was at the urging of the student member that letters requesting submissions to the committee were addressed to each student as well as to faculty members, and in terms of the committee's reputation and credibility among students this seems to have been a most important move. Every committee member I interviewed referred to the frequent and important interjection of a student point of view in the committee deliberations. A precise cause-and-effect relationship cannot be demonstrated, but it seems likely that the important student support which the study subsequently received may in some degree have been a result of the fact that it reflected student concerns.

Several members of the committee suggested that they did not have sufficient time for the job they were given to do, and it was at least implied that this was the reason for a lack of discussion of general principles. It also seems clear that the chairman was not in favor of including such a discussion.

During its work the committee maintained a great deal of contact with the rest of the university. Much of this contact was maintained to get information and feedback, and some for essentially political purposes. However, the committee generally agreed that after its report appeared it would not take an active role in the processes of consideration and implementation. Some members served as resource persons for subsequent review committees, but none were active in council debates. Professor Macpherson, especially, remained in the background.

**SUMMARY OF THE RECOM- MENDATIONS** The report of the Macpherson Committee included four main chapters: "Teaching and Learning," "The Structure of Degree Programs," "The Colleges," and "The Undergraduate and His Environment." Ninety-eight specific recommendations were made under these headings. Some called for specific action by the top administration. Some called for legislation by the faculty, and others for action by the departments. Some were essentially exhortations addressed to various individuals or groups. A number of recommendations, especially in the last two chapters, related to matters relevant only in the particular context of Toronto. The basic intent of the more general recommendations is summarized below.

**Teaching and Learning** The report included a rather sweeping, generalized discussion of teaching and learning and recommended that undergraduate teaching be more suitably and obviously rewarded. This was backed up by proposals for the use of student evaluations of teachers and courses and for the inspection, by senior faculty members, of the classes of junior teachers. Both of these would be used in departmental decisions about faculty promotion and the like. More organized attention by departments to the development, as teachers, of younger faculty members and teaching assistants was proposed, and more control and supervision of the latter were recommended.

The committee made further, and rather unique, recommendations about the processes of teaching. Among these was that more than one lecture per week in any course be prohibited. Part of the time previously devoted to lecturing would be given over to tutorials of not more than 10 or 12 students. It was also recommended that tutorials in the first year be given by senior faculty members, leaving teaching assistants to handle those in the upper years. But not all the released time would be used, for it was recommended that a student carrying five subjects (the normal practice at Toronto) would have no more than 10 hours per week—exclusive of laboratories—in the classroom. The number of laboratory periods in relevant courses would be cut in half.

The committee also proposed a major deemphasis on examinations.[2] In the first year, it was proposed that no more than one-half of the course grade should be based on the examination. Examinations at the end of the second year would be completely eliminated, while at the end of the third year they would move as far as possible in the direction of being comprehensive examinations covering more than one year.

**Curriculum**  In terms of past Toronto practice, the recommendations concerning curriculum were extremely radical. Basically, they called for a very major upgrading of the status and conduct of the general program. They did not, of course, call for a downgrading of the honours program, but short of a tremendous increase in available resources, it seems clear that some redirection of effort would inevitably follow adoption of these recommendations.

The committee proposed uniform admission and passing standards for all students. Students would no longer be required to commit themselves to the generalist or specialist program upon entrance, and the distinction between general and honours students in the first year would be abolished. As the report put it, "Generalists and specialists should sit together in some of the same classes." The committee called for "basic courses" in each department for all students and for "combined courses," as, for example, in physical sciences. Finally, "collateral courses" were proposed in fields such as mathematics and English for those who want or need less rigorous work and do not intend to do further work in these areas. The committee also proposed a first-year distribution requirement. The student's choice of five first-year courses would have to be spread

---

[2] Examinations have traditionally been more important in Canada than in the United States. At least until recently, it has not been uncommon for the grade in a course to rest entirely on the final examination.

over at least two of the three traditional divisions, and no more than two courses in any one division would be permitted. The committee also proposed a number of technical arrangements which would have the effect of preventing departments from thwarting the much freer first year by imposing departmental or course prerequisites.

In general, the intent of the curriculum proposals was to introduce a considerably greater degree of student choice in addition to achieving a significant elimination of the many distinctions between the general and honours programs. Also, the recommendations had the effect of lessening the power of individual departments to prescribe programs for students.

With respect to the administration of the curriculum, the committee proposed to have an associate dean for each division of the faculty. In addition, each division would have two program directors responsible for oversight of the specialist programs. While it was intended that these directors would remain part-time teachers, they would not be responsible to their department chairmen for their work as program directors. Their recommendations would be reviewed only by a new standing committee made up of the dean, associate deans, and the program directors. This same committee would be the standing committee for the general program. The intent of all these recommendations for administrative changes was to provide some offset to the power of the specialized departments in the administration of curriculum.

Beyond these recommendations, and largely to assuage the unhappiness of some committee members with the absence of any discussion of educational philosophy and objectives, creation of a committee to study the longer-range relationship of the specialist and generalist educational programs to a liberal education was recommended.

Most of the recommendations relating to the colleges arose from the peculiar structure of Toronto and were largely technical in nature. Essentially, the committee wanted to "restore the reality of the old colleges as academic communities serving all their students." To do this, it proposed to remove some of the traditional independence of the colleges by eliminating the several departments in the college-based subjects and thereby putting all subjects and departments on a university-wide basis. At the same time, the colleges, as teaching units, would be broadened by having them give collegiate instruction in a much broader spectrum of university subjects. Faculty members would, in effect, have joint appointments in the university department and in one of the colleges. The committees concluded that "the old colleges can become real communities to their students only if they do some significant amount of teaching of all, or as nearly as possible all, of their students, and . . . this requires that they do some of the teaching in what are now university subjects."

**Student Relations**  The Macpherson Committee recommended rather widespread incorporation of students into the decision-making processes of the university. Departmental student-faculty committees which would be effective decision-making bodies on matters relating to curriculum and teaching were proposed, as were student representatives as full members of the Council of the Faculty of Arts and Sciences and its committees. More faculty office hours and student-faculty common rooms in academic buildings were also suggested. (It should be recalled that the changes proposed in the college structure would also make possible greater student and faculty contact.)

In the matter of student advising, the committee concluded that its recommendations for simplifying the curricula would be a major help since the student would be faced with far fewer complexities to comprehend. It also recommended that each department have supervisors of undergraduate studies who would spend an important part of their time advising students. Time thus spent would be equaled by a reduction in teaching commitments.

**OVERALL IMPACT OF THE RECOM-MENDATIONS**  The recommendations of the Macpherson Committee called for some extremely radical departures from Toronto practice and tradition. The recommended downgrading of the lecture system —perhaps more firmly entrenched at Toronto than in most American universities—would, if implemented, make a highly significant change in the university. The emphasis on smaller classes, fewer classes, and the greater involvement of senior faculty members in lower-division teaching was less dramatic than the downgrading of lecturing, but if seriously implemented, these recommendations would result in potentially significant change. The changes in curriculum—especially those which would put honours and general programs on the same footing —represented an almost complete overturn of decades of tradition. That the proposed system—much more nearly a free elective system—is less dramatic in the American context should not obscure its radicalism in the Toronto context. Finally, the several recommendations for serious student involvement in university and departmental decision making were, in the context of early 1967, almost revolutionary. This is especially the case since, on the whole, Canadian students had not been radicalized by either Vietnam war protests or the civil rights movement.

CONSIDERA-
TION OF
THE RECOM-
MENDATIONS

The Macpherson report did not reach the faculty and students until late in 1967, when both the president and Professor Macpherson were on leave from the campus. Professor Macpherson had discussed the handling of the report with President Bissell after the latter had reviewed a draft of it and had indicated his essential agreement with its substance. The president and the chairman agreed that the entire report should not be submitted to the faculty during the president's absence but that the departments might begin to implement recommendations directed toward them. In the broader context of the university, however, it appears that allowing the report to sit for a year was, in the words of one senior administrator, a "nondecision."

After the report came out, it was the subject of a considerable amount of attention and discussion. Opposition centered on what was seen as an attempt to undercut departmental autonomy. Opposition to the meshing of the honours and general programs was centered in the classics and English departments. (It should be recalled that these were "college departments.") Curiously, much of the opposition to the report—and especially to its recommendations concerning teaching and learning—came from American or American-trained faculty members. There appear to be two reasons for this. One was based on the typical experience in larger American universities that maintenance of small classes (seminars, tutorials, and the like) inevitably means that more of the teaching is done by teaching assistants, since there are simply not enough regular faculty members to go around. The other reason is that these Americans were attracted to Toronto because of the high degree of specialization involved in the honours programs. As noted earlier, these were far more specialized than the usual American undergraduate program.

After the report came out, Dean Allen of the Faculty of Arts and Sciences concluded that it would achieve nothing if not given some push. He therefore asked each department to consider the report (and urged that students be involved) and to report to him by

Christmas. He finally received all the reports in the spring and at that time formed an ad hoc committee to pull together formal proposals for faculty action. This committee, during May and June of 1968, reviewed the reports of the departments (which dealt primarily with matters concerning teaching and curriculum), discussed many aspects of these submissions with departmental members, and prepared a series of legislative proposals to be submitted to the council in September.

In the interim, student demands for a voice in university decision making had become extreme, and in what seems to be an almost universal pattern, neither the administration nor the faculty was really prepared to deal with them. Consequently, there was a roomful of students at the first meeting of the council called to consider the report of Dean Allen's ad hoc committee. (The meeting was conducted with several students sitting on the floor under the table at which the dean and other officials sat.) Needless to say, little business was done. A second meeting was called and met with the same protest. At this point the dean, along with some key faculty members and students, put together a resolution calling for an entirely new subcommittee to consider the Macpherson report. The key feature of this resolution was that it would consist of one faculty member and one student chosen from each department. The clear intent of the resolution was to prevent the student power issue in overall terms from keeping the university from proceeding with implementation of the Macpherson recommendations. In a meeting of the faculty on October 9, 1968, this resolution was overwhelmingly passed and carried the support of all but the most militant students.

The Committee of Fifty, as it came to be known, was quickly formed. Dean Allen commented that in the absence of any plans for such an occurrence, the election of students took place under most chaotic conditions and that the whole thing could have been disastrous. He suggested, however, that virtually everyone saw himself involved in "a something or nothing occasion" to achieve some of the reforms proposed by the Macpherson commission. The Committee of Fifty met every night for two weeks and hammered out proposals which were introduced in the council. The provost conducted most of the council meetings which dealt with the proposals, and all agreed that he conducted these difficult meetings firmly but fairly. The student members of the council contributed a great deal of support. Dean Allen stated that some of them were "magnificent throughout." With some modification, the proposals were accepted by the council.

OVERALL
RESULTS

In Professor Macpherson's view these actions represented an "underimplementation of Chapter 2" (Teaching and Learning) and an "overimplementation of Chapter 3" (Curriculum). Basically, the recommendations adopted did eliminate all distinctions between the honours and the general programs except for the difference in length of time. (At the time of this writing, it appeared possible that Ontario might phase out its grade 13 in high school and that both honours and general would then become four-year programs after grade 12.) The curriculum finally adopted eliminated the modest distribution requirement proposed by the Macpherson Committee and made the undergraduate program completely elective. In essence, the university now has prescribed honours and general programs which the student may elect to follow, but he may forego such election and define his own course of study completely. In terms of entrance requirements, academic standing, and degree requirement all distinctions between general and honours students were eliminated. Quite naturally, attention of the council was focused on the first two years, but it is likely that the different degrees will eventually be eliminated. Action on these proposals was completed in time to permit the new program to begin in September, 1969.

The other recommendations of the Macpherson report relating to teaching and learning were left largely to the departments for implementation. There was a general feeling that the recommended tutorials and other small class arrangements were simply beyond the university's resources, and large numbers of faculty members and students were not convinced that all courses should be subject to blanket prescriptions about teaching formats.

In essence, however, the new curriculum regulations did achieve about a 25 percent reduction in normal class hours, and the amount of laboratory time, as the Macpherson report recommended, was generally cut in half. Recommendations concerning examinations were left with individual departments.

In the sense that the Macpherson recommendations were designed to provide for restraints on the autonomy of departments, the report was not accepted. However, Dean Allen observed that part of the process of consideration and implementation had been the widespread incorporation of students into the deliberations and decision making of departments. He feels that students will continue to be involved, and as he put it, "Once this happens, you can relax the watchdog role. Students will take care of themselves." He pointed out that when the Macpherson report was started, everyone greatly feared the power of departments to thwart change. (Except, presumably, the power of one's own department.) However, the Macpherson report had brought about great changes—largely through departments—and this, in Dean Allen's view, resulted from the involvement of students. Other faculty members shared the dean's view, but not all were quite so sanguine about the long-run efficaciousness of student involvement. Nearly everyone commented on the tremendous amount of time being consumed in endless faculty-student meetings.

In the spring of 1969, most of the other recommendations of the Macpherson Committee—many of which involved action by university administration in addition to, or in lieu of, action by the Faculty of Arts and Sciences—had not been considered. Nor did there appear to be any urgency to consider them. One has the impression that the widespread upheaval of the previous winter and autumn and the sudden involvement of students made almost everyone want to wait and see what would happen. The recommendations about the federated colleges had political implications which ran deep and wide both within and outside the university, and direct confrontation of these issues may be impossible in any case.

**COMMENTARY**   The Macpherson Committee report resulted in some very major changes in the educational policies of the University of Toronto. While consideration of the report, let alone action taken, was very spotty in terms of the broad scope of the recommendations, those changes finally enacted are at least as far-reaching in terms of where Toronto was when the process began as those of any other institution reviewed in this study.

It is tempting to say that student power, constructively exercised, carried the day at Toronto, but to do so would be to ignore the prescience of President Bissell in inaugurating the study, the provocative but realistic recommendations of the report, and, above all, the important exercise of leadership by Dean Allen after the report came out. All these were equally necessary to the process of change, but I sense that the students were more equal than the others. I first visited Toronto in connection with this study in October, 1968, on the day the formation of the Committee of Fifty was approved. I came away from my visit with the impression that while there was a general acceptance of much of the Macpherson report, there was far less enthusiasm for really doing anything about it. Very few, I sensed, were willing to engage in the effort to try to overcome the various pockets of self-interest which so often act to preclude much change in a university. The lack of discussion of educational philosophy in the report and its lack of passionate rhetoric, of any "call to arms," were given as criticisms of it and seemed almost to provide an apology for not doing very much about it. One might well have concluded at that time that the Macpherson report was a dead issue. When I returned to Toronto in early April, 1969, the atmosphere was quite different, mainly because things had been accomplished: people had gone through a real effort to compromise conflicting interest. The one significant change in the overall situation in the university between October and April was the greatly increased involvement of students in its deliberative process. At the very least, it appears that student involvement gave the push which permitted consideration of the Macpherson report to get off dead center and be carried through in what, for a large university, is a remarkably short time.

On the other hand, one may suggest that the success of the Macpherson report was the result of Dean Allen's decision to make the departments (with or without students) the center of the process of consideration. It does seem certain that this would not have worked without the dean's effective prodding of the departments, but with this prodding, the departments did the job, and it seems that many of the contentious issues were largely worked out before reaching the formal legislative stage. But the working out was done through Dean Allen and his several committees. There was no assumption that action would bubble up from the departments if they were left to their own devices. The fires under them were regularly rekindled. However, this process does appear to have prevented the occurrence of the kinds of direct confrontation of special interests which probably would have resulted from introducing the report into the council in the beginning.

One final comment about student involvement is in order. I believe, as one well over 30, that the changes in the curricula which were made are much less significant, *from the point of view of students,* than the proposals about teaching and learning which were not generally accepted.[3] Though changes in the content of education are needed, it seems to me that students will, on the whole, be better served by significant changes in its processes. Perhaps students see this differently from the way I do, or perhaps the Toronto students were, in a sense, co-opted by the faculty. The changes in the Toronto curricula will require some changes in *what* the faculty does—but in a very real sense they will give the faculty member a chance to "do his own thing." The tightly prescribed honours programs, unlike an elective system, gave the faculty member little opportunity to "teach his Ph.D. dissertation." Now he may well be able to do so. On the other hand, the changes regarding teaching and learning would have required some very fundamental changes in the *way* in which most faculty members behave, and these changes have largely not been implemented, though they may eventually be brought about through the departments.

In essence, I am suggesting that the changes made at Toronto are, on the whole, those which will involve the least change in the attitude and behavior of most faculty members. Those proposals which would have required very much more of such changes have generally been put aside.

Having said the foregoing, I must repeat that, overall, the changes brought about at Toronto were significant, even though they appear to have resulted less from any planned process than from the seizure and effective use of opportunities presented by the flow of events.

---

[3] I should perhaps add that I taught in Canada (not at Toronto) for a number of years and am profoundly amazed at the apparent scope of the curriculum changes which were made. They are truly revolutionary.

# 5. Swarthmore College

## Critique of a College

Swarthmore College is widely recognized as one of America's distinguished liberal arts colleges. Its student body, which is very carefully selected for academic ability, numbers just over 1,000. Slightly more than half are men. Most Swarthmore graduates go on to graduate school and careers in the academic world or in other professions. The faculty members, whose average salaries are among the highest in the country, number about 125. In contrast to the typical national experience, Swarthmore has not experienced uncontrolled growth in the past decade or so. Except for an engineering program which is quite small, Swarthmore's curriculum is confined to the traditional liberal arts and sciences. Only a very limited amount of graduate work at the master's level has been offered.

Faculty participation in college government at Swarthmore was, in 1966, carried on basically by the faculty meeting as a body and through a traditional structure of faculty committees. The college had the usual departmental structure, and the departments were loosely organized into divisions, though these latter did not play an important role in the governmental processes. Faculty meetings were chaired by the president and, as in many small colleges, presidential authority was strong. All appointments to departmental chairmanships, committees, and the like were made by the president.

The Commission on Educational Policy was established by President Courtney C. Smith in the summer of 1966 and began its work in the fall of that year. The commission worked through the summer of 1967, and in November of 1967 its report was published along with the reports of two other special committees: one on library policy and one on student life. (Only the report of the Commission on Educational Policy is considered here.)

During December and January the report was discussed by four groups—including all faculty members, administrators, and student representatives—which were especially created for this purpose. Through this process, the commission made some modifications in its recommendations prior to the report's being formally introduced into the faculty meeting beginning in February.

The faculty met weekly during February and March and twice each week beginning in April. By the end of the academic year in June, 1968, all the commission's recommendations had been acted upon by the faculty. Most were approved. Changes which required approval by the college's Board of Managers had also been acted upon by late June, and in the summer and fall of 1968 the college began to implement the changes made.

**ORIGIN OF THE STUDY** The decision to undertake a wide-ranging study of Swarthmore's educational policies appears to have been made in response to three different concerns. The first of these was about the ability of Swarthmore to continue to attract and to keep on its faculty persons with an orientation toward research. This concern was expressed in a letter to President Smith signed by several faculty members—mostly in the sciences and including younger members. None of the group who wrote the letter appears to have felt that Swarthmore should attempt to depart from its traditional role as an undergraduate liberal arts college, but there was sufficient concern about the loss of some faculty members to universities with graduate work and a research orientation to lead the group to ask President Smith for a broad inquiry into Swarthmore's educational policies as they related to research activities.

The second concern was somewhat broader in nature. In 1922, under President Frank Aydelotte, Swarthmore introduced its famous honors program, which is characterized by intense investigation of a subject area, close faculty-student collaboration, and examination of students by outsiders (*Faculty of Swarthmore College,* 1942).

This program was a major innovation in American undergraduate education and has been often admired, if not imitated, by others. At the same time that one group of faculty members became concerned about the climate for research at Swarthmore, others began to talk about a number of rigidities which were contrary to the original spirit of the honors program but which these faculty members felt had nevertheless come to characterize its operation.

Out of these discussions there emerged a more general conclusion that the college had operated for some time without any major review or changes. As one of them said, "The curriculum committee was keeping the machinery going, but never got around to a major overhaul." In general, the group felt that no one in the college was thinking seriously about educational policy. These concerns led a small group of faculty members to address a letter to President Smith suggesting a far-ranging examination of the college's educational policies by a group of outsiders—an investigation patterned after that of the Franks Committee at Oxford. The faculty members who sent this letter were simply a group of good friends, and they made no attempt to enlist college-wide support—to turn the letter into a petition.

These two letters reached President Smith at a moment when he was convinced of the need for a basic reexamination of the college's educational policies and of the relationships between the college and its students. This conviction had developed during the preceding year, when he had had a chance to view events in American higher education generally from the perspective of a leave in England. Essentially, the two letters indicated to President Smith that he would have faculty support, and so he moved quickly to get these investigations under way. He announced that the Commission on Educational Policy (C.E.P.), as well as the other committees on student life and library policy, would be called into being promptly.

The two letters to the president were conceived of and sent quite independently, but it is clear that in one way or another they struck a responsive chord in the Swarthmore faculty generally, for the president's announcement was received enthusiastically. One signer of the second letter stated that faculty response was far more enthusiastic than he and his colleagues had anticipated. Initial student reaction was rather skeptical and generally involved an assumption that nothing much would come of such a study.

**MAKEUP OF THE COMMISSION** It is the tradition of Swarthmore that members of committees are chosen by the president, and this tradition was followed in the case of the C.E.P. The idea of a commission made up entirely of outsiders—proposed in one of the letters—was never given serious consideration by the president, although the involvement of some external members was accepted from the outset. President Smith stated that external members are absolutely necessary in such a case because they can pick up and challenge the unstated assumptions that are generally a part of the thinking of any group within a particular institution.

President Smith consulted with a number of people in selecting faculty members of the commission. In making his appointments to the commission, he made no attempt to provide for the traditional balance among groups of disciplines—to get a sort of mirror representation of the faculty as a whole. He stated that he wished to appoint people who had real concerns about education and who had the capacity to draw others in. The chairman of the commission was appointed first, and then he and the president agreed on the next appointment, and so on until the five faculty members were chosen. The external members were primarily the choices of President Smith, although they were selected after the internal members had been appointed and consulted by the president. Four of the faculty members were among the signers of one or the other of the two letters sent to President Smith. As one faculty member— not on the committee—observed, "All members of the commission were scholars and teachers of high standing, and all were beyond reproach in terms of their integrity." Details of commission membership are given in Table 4, which shows that the commission included neither really junior faculty members, in terms of rank or of service on the Swarthmore faculty, nor "Aydelotte men"—senior faculty members who had been at Swarthmore during the presidency of Frank Aydelotte. As another faculty member, not on the commission, put it, "The commission members were vigorous,

**TABLE 4** *Membership of the Commission on Educational Policy, Swarthmore College*

| Name and rank | Field | Age group* | Years at Swarthmore | Degrees from Swarthmore |
|---|---|---|---|---|
| Monroe Beardsley, professor | Philosophy | 50–57 | 22 | None |
| James Field, professor | History | 50–57 | 22 | None |
| Charles Gilbert, associate professor | Political science | 42–49 | 16 | None |
| Kermit Gordon, outside member† | | 34–41 | | A. B. |
| Mark Heald, associate professor | Physics | 34–41 | 10 | None |
| Samuel Hynes, professor | English | 42–49 | 19 | None |
| Winnifred Pierce, outside member† | | | | A.B. |
| Robert Sproul, outside member | | | | None |

*Ages and years at the institution are given as of the time the committee was first convened.
†Member of Swarthmore Board of Managers.

concerned men who were seen neither as establishment or young-sters."

It seems clear that the makeup of the commission was well received by virtually all members of the Swarthmore community and that its eventual recommendations were bound to carry weight.

**CONDUCT OF THE STUDY** The commission worked without specific terms of reference but with a general understanding that it would review the entire academic program of Swarthmore College. The only constraints on the scope of the commission's inquiry were the simultaneous examinations of student life and library policy being made by separate committees. In the preamble to its report, the commission stated that in its early meeting a focus on three basic elements was established: "(1) curriculum and instruction; (2) issues relating to the faculty; and (3) questions of institutional function and structure integral to the first two. [In addition,] we further acknowledged our concern about the problems and potentials, the institutional goals and social role, of our kind of college."

Appendix A of *Critique of a College* includes a quite detailed description of the commission's procedures, and those details need not be repeated here. The commission worked entirely openly from the beginning. Faculty members and students were invited to make submissions to the commission about anything and everything. A number of questionnaire surveys of the views of students, alumni, and outside honors examiners were made, and a number of these people were formally interviewed. There was no student membership on the commission, but a Student Curriculum Committee made its own investigations of many matters which were part of the commission's purview, and there was close and regular communication between the commission and the student group throughout the study. In essence, these procedures ensured that everyone in the college was more or less constantly aware of the commission's existence and that a great many were, in one way or another, involved in its work.

The commission averaged about 20 hours per week at its work during the academic year, and all members spent full time on the study during the summer of 1967. The outside members of the commission had been engaged by President Smith to spend one weekend each month in session with the commission. In addition to this they were expected to read the various position papers, drafts, research reports, and so forth which the commission prepared or had prepared. The faculty members of the commission all agreed that the outside members worked very seriously and very hard at their jobs and made an important contribution to the commission, although the faculty members periodically lost momentum through having to devote a certain amount of time to bringing the outside members up to date when the latter rejoined the group. The principal value of the external members was in forcing the faculty members to recognize that a number of their assumptions were, in fact, just that.

The evidence from interviews with faculty members, and indeed from the internal consistency of the report itself, is that the commission became a very effective working group. All members of the commission clearly have a great deal of respect for the chairman, and he obviously influenced the way in which the commission operated and presented its final report. One member of the commission reported that the chairman maintained a perspective on the whole task and led the commission into considering the right details at precisely the right time.

In only two cases did the commission discuss its more or less final conclusions with others prior to publication of the report. A draft of the report was read by President Smith and discussed by the commission and him prior to printing. The president made a few suggestions for changes in the substance of the report on the basis of his own experience and knowledge. The commission accepted certain of these changes and did not accept others. It is clear that none of these were matters of serious contention.

Several of the report's recommendations would directly affect the work of individual departments, but the recommendations concerning foreign languages could be viewed as especially threatening to the departments involved. Consequently, the relevant part of the text was shown to and discussed with the members of that department. As a result of these discussions the commission made some changes in its recommendations.

In its own work, the commission apparently spent little time discussing educational principles. The chairman initially pushed the committee toward immediate discussion of specific problems. The first chapters of the final report include extensive discussions of educational philosophy generally and of the nature and function of the small college, but apparently these were derived from the preponderance of the conclusions reached by the commission about specific issues rather than from any kind of a priori reasoning.

It appears that relatively little compromising, as opposed to achieving consensus, was involved in the preparation of the commission's final report. There is no evidence that any member of the commission became an adamant minority on any aspect of its recommendations. The report did include a formal minority position on the amount of reduction in honors papers, but it was stated that this was done primarily to give the full faculty the alternative to consider.

All faculty members of the commission indicated that there were parts of the report with which they were not in full agreement but that the full report was the unanimous product of all the members of the commission, with perhaps one exception—the section of the report dealing with engineering. By most conventional standards, an engineering program is somewhat out of place in a college like Swarthmore. It is an expensive operation and involves relatively few students. Some members of the commission felt that it would be best all around if the engineering program at Swarthmore were eliminated. Others felt that this should not be done or, as a practical matter, that it could not be done. Thus the recommendations relating to engineering are a fairly tightly written compromise of these opposing views. In connection with the practical aspects of the engineering question, commission members stated that this was the only point on which commission views were in any way modified by consideration of "what could get by." With this exception, the commission's recommendations were made without any compromise with real or imagined institutional politics.[1]

One final aspect of the commission's procedures was that, from the beginning, President Smith made it quite clear to the commission—and to everyone else—that he was committed to publishing whatever the commission came up with as a final report. Several members suggested that this commitment contributed greatly to the effectiveness of the commission's work.

**SUMMARY OF THE RECOMMENDATIONS** *Critique of a College* included 165 separate recommendations. A great range of topics was touched upon, and the overall impor-

[1] In evaluating these statements by commission members, it is well to recognize that since at least the internal members were of the institution and regular participants in its politics, unknowing accommodations may have been made. All the internal members of the commission were part of a small, intimate community and had been so for a relatively long time. It is perhaps unlikely that their collective views would, for the most part, be very different from those of the community generally.

tance of the recommendations varied considerably. Many recommendations were technical in nature or were related to situations unique to Swarthmore. The summary which follows deals with those recommendations which are of general applicability.

**General Curriculum**

Several recommendations taken together add up to a widespread loosening of basic curriculum requirements, although any departure from the basic structure of courses, instructors, grades, semesters, and the like was specifically rejected. It was proposed that the normal course load during the first two years be reduced from 18 to 16 courses and that students be freely permitted to graduate in less than four years. Opportunities for independent study would be broadened, and each student would be permitted to undertake one independent research project during the first two years. Student- or faculty-initiated ad hoc courses would be permitted, and student-run courses without a faculty member carrying on instruction would be possible. Students would be permitted to "attach" additional work for additional credit to regular courses, while in the other direction, courses running over only half a semester would be encouraged. Up to one semester's credit would be given for practical work done away from the campus.

The commission recommended retaining the distribution-requirement approach to general education. The Swarthmore requirement involved at least two courses in each of four groups: (1) natural science; (2) literature, art history, and music; (3) history, philosophy, and psychology; and (4) economics, political science, and sociology-anthropology. The courses were picked from a prescribed list, and a further constraint was that they must be chosen from at least six departments. However, the committee recommended that the general language requirement be eliminated and that the distribution requirement not be confined to the first two years. It was also recommended that all freshman-year courses be graded on a pass-fail basis only. In addition, specific distribution requirements could be met by examination or by advanced placement standing.

**Honors Program**

At the beginning of their junior year, Swarthmore students enter either the honors program or the course program. The latter is essentially similar to the programs found in virtually all colleges and universities and involves a departmental major. Honors students:

. . . prepare for eight examinations ("papers"), which are set and graded solely by external examiners. The standard method of preparation is centered on small, weekly seminars, of which average size is about six and the upper limit is eight. Thus honors students take about half the range of subjects carried by course students, though at about twice the intensity: wide reading in original sources is encouraged. A typical honors student's program consists of four seminars and papers in a major department and two in each of two minors, though many variations are possible. About 45 percent of juniors enter the honors program and about 35 percent graduate in it (Sw., 1967, p. 102).

The essential characteristics of the honors program have been the external examination, the intensive exploration of a field, and small group instruction. It was the feeling of the commission that the latter, especially, had become too much the norm—that in a sense, form had assumed a greater importance than function. There was a further feeling that the content of many of the seminars had become much too tightly prescribed and that having the entire upper-division years confined to honors (for those enrolled in the program) was too restrictive.

The commission's recommendations were aimed primarily at loosening some of these rigidities. It proposed that students be examined by external examiners on only three-quarters of the work of the last two years. It was further proposed that a detailed description of the course of study for a paper be prepared—the intent being to shift emphasis away from the methods and toward the ends of preparation. It was recommended that the seminar be abandoned as the usual method of preparation for papers. Students would be allowed, under the commission's proposals, to enter the honors program at the beginning of the sophomore and senior years, as well as at the start of the junior year. Honors students taking "courses" would be graded in these on a pass-fail basis.

The principal changes recommended for the course program were the establishment of interdepartmental programs and problem-oriented or topical programs in the senior year.

**Other Programs** An important series of recommendations called for the introduction of work in the creative arts at Swarthmore. Work in virtually all the arts was proposed, and the addition of faculty and facilities to make this possible was recommended. Initially, academic credit granted for work in the creative arts would be limited to the equivalent of four courses. There is an implication in the commission's discussions that granting of credit for work in the creative arts might be expanded after the college had gained some experience in offering work in this area.

As noted above, the commission recommended that the general language requirement be abolished, although departments would be permitted to establish such requirements. Simultaneously, a number of proposals were made to strengthen language instruction, such as the employment of more native speakers, greater use of language laboratories, and more utilization of language skills in other areas. In the sciences, the commission recommended a redesign of curricula to permit more work outside the sciences and to create more opportunities for independent laboratory work. A series of recommendations were made to achieve a liberalization or deprofessionalization of the engineering program.

**Graduate Work and Research**    Except for an occasional master's degree almost always awarded to students whose undergraduate work had been done at Swarthmore, the college did not offer graduate work. It will be recalled that one of the letters to President Smith which led to the establishment of the commission was concerned with the lack of graduate work and research. The commission made a thorough analysis of faculty turnover and concluded that Swarthmore had not lost many faculty members for this reason. On the other hand, the commission had little doubt that it was becoming increasingly difficult for a college to attract and keep highly qualified faculty members in the face of competition from research-oriented universities. To meet this problem the commission recommended that more time and opportunity for faculty research be provided by means of reduced teaching loads, less committee work, and support of academic leave for research. The commission also recommended some expansion of masters' programs and the establishment of research institutes on the campus. Perhaps most important—potentially, at any rate—was the recommendation:

That Swarthmore College explore the possibility of formal arrangements with the University of Pennsylvania and Temple University to facilitate graduate teaching and research opportunities for faculty members on a released time basis, as well as reciprocal teaching and research opportunities at the College for staff and graduate students of the universities.

This obviously represents an ingenious attempt to preserve the character of Swarthmore as a small liberal arts college, while simultaneously meeting the needs of the contemporary professor for more than the collegiate scene offers.

**Administration**  A central proposal by the commission was the appointment of a provost who would have a key role in academic administration and act as the president's principal adviser in academic affairs. The commission's intent was to provide a counterforce to the tendencies toward decentralization, fragmentation, and excessive departmentalization, which were in evidence at Swarthmore as elsewhere, though to a very much lesser degree. A principal function of the provost would be to provide a focus for long-range planning. In addition, the provost would chair an elected Council on Educational Policy, which would be a principal advisory group for the president. Clearly, the commission was suggesting that new administrative arrangements were necessary to carry out the many changes it proposed.

Like so many of the self-study groups, the Swarthmore commission found that the college had remarkably little information available about what it was doing and had done. Consequently, it made a series of recommendations to bring about the collection, retention, and use of more and better data about students and academic matters generally.

**OVERALL IMPACT OF THE PROPOSALS**  Except in the case of recommendations concerning honors and those relating to faculty research, the proposals made by the Commission on Educational Policy for changes at Swarthmore did not represent a sharp break from the past. Changes in the areas of languages and engineering were difficult because they spoke directly to the work of individuals. In the case of honors, the proposals did call for some very specific changes in practice—for the undermining of several decades of practice. With the adoption of these proposals, many Swarthmore faculty members would have to make important changes in their behavior.

The striking difference between the general drift of the Swarthmore recommendations and that of most of the other studies reviewed is that the concern at Swarthmore is with freeing up faculty time *for* research, while most of the other institutions are concerned with shaking faculty loose *from* research. This difference is undoubtedly a reflection of the fact that Swarthmore is a small liberal arts college without the superstructure of a professional graduate school. Swarthmore appears, in any case, to be taking some tentative steps toward joining the Academic Revolution, from whose extremes others are perhaps trying to draw back.

The full report, along with the reports of the library and student life committees, was published at the end of November, 1967, and copies were given to all faculty members and all students. As one member of the commission pointed out, giving the report to all the students immediately "set them up." As soon as the report came out, the decision was made to suspend all classes, seminars, laboratories, and other regularly scheduled activities for a week. During this week, which has come in the Swarthmore tradition to be known as Super Week, the student council arranged many formal and informal meetings for discussion of the report. It is clear that Super Week gave everyone, students and faculty alike, the undeniable feeling of participation, and along with this an undeniable feeling that nothing was being railroaded. At the conclusion of Super Week the faculty began consideration of the details of the report.

During the summer preceding publication of *Critique of a College,* Dean Susan P. Cobbs and some other members of the Swarthmore administration and faculty had been participants in a Danforth conference on college administration. Each institutional group at the conference had to develop a topic for consideration by participants, and the Swarthmore group, knowing that the college would soon receive the report of the Commission on Educational Policy, addressed itself to the problem of getting effective faculty consideration of a series of proposals for major changes. As a result of this effort, Dean Cobbs and her group proposed a series of discussions by smaller groups prior to the introduction of specific proposals into the regular legislative processes of the faculty. Four such groups were created and included students, faculty members, and administrators. Faculty members and administrators were assigned to the groups by means of computer selection designed to achieve a balance of age and fields in each group.[2] Student members were elected from department majors. The only purpose of the Danforth Groups (as they came to be known) was to discuss informally the commission's recommendations. No decisions or reports were expected or required. It was hoped that through this

[2] Dean Cobbs had originally proposed combining academic departments into four groups, but the faculty opted for random membership.

process, questions of fact, intention, and interpretation would be cleared up and, in the words of President Smith, that "the opening volley that would have done little more than expose visceral reactions" would be kept out of the actual decision-making process. The groups met about once a week during December and January. The student members of the Danforth Groups were in regular communication with the student body, and there was considerable feedback from the students.

In February, formal faculty consideration of the recommendations began. There was something of a flare-up over the question of student attendance and participation at the faculty meetings. The faculty voted not to invite students to attend, and some students became quite upset. However, some of the student leaders stated that student concern quickly dissipated because it was obvious that the faculty was going to accept most of the report anyway.

The Instruction Committee of the Faculty (a standing committee) acted as floor manager for the report. An agenda subcommittee headed by Dean Cobbs worked closely with the commission in preparing the agenda for each meeting. On the basis of the discussions in the Danforth Groups, the commission reworded some of its proposals and withdrew some. Related recommendations — regardless of where they appeared in the report — were grouped together for discussion, and the items known to be most controversial were taken up first. Members of the commission directed the discussion of each agenda item. In April, when it became apparent that weekly meetings of the faculty would not permit consideration of all recommendations before June, a schedule of twice-weekly meetings was instituted. Almost all faculty members attended almost all meetings, and by the end of the academic year in June, all the commission's recommendations had been considered, and most had been accepted by the college faculty.

Faculty members stated that during this entire period of intense discussion, President Smith was completely in control. One member said that he was patient and courteous, but always forceful, and that there was never any doubt of his basic support of the commission's proposals. All faculty members appear to have had ample opportunity to make known their views on each of the proposals. The usual number of impassioned speeches for or against (mostly the latter) occurred at several faculty meetings, but as one faculty member put it, this was mostly talking through an open door.

Several suggested that as a result of the intensive discussions during Super Week and the Danforth meetings and because of the small size of the Swarthmore faculty, most of the necessary compromises on specifics had been worked out to the satisfaction of a substantial majority before the recommendations came to the floor. In short, by the time of voting, widespread agreement had been reached on most of the recommendations.

**OVERALL RESULTS** As indicated above, all the recommendations of the commission had been considered by the Swarthmore faculty by June, 1968, and implementation was well under way in the fall of 1968. The recommendation for the appointment of a provost was accepted, but because President Smith announced his intention to resign at the end of the academic year 1968–69, it was agreed that the post would not be filled until a new president had been appointed. The proposal for dropping the general language requirement was temporarily shelved although it is likely that it will be implemented in the future. Otherwise, the recommendations of the commission were accepted as made or with minor modification.

In the shorter perspective, the Swarthmore study achieved a great deal. Students, faculty, and administration were brought together in a shared enterprise. A number of quite significant changes were proposed, and most were ultimately accepted by virtually everyone, including those who would be affected by them. However, many of the changes proposed involved changes in approaches and attitudes rather than changes in rules, and a longer perspective is undoubtedly necessary to test results.

It was only at this longer-run level that I encountered any uncertainty about the efficacy of what had been achieved. Some older faculty members expressed a fear that change might go too far. One such person suggested that the commission was intended from the beginning to break up some of the rigidities that had come to characterize "the older Swarthmore." He wondered whether that had not begun to have happened even before the commission began its work under the impact of newer faculty members, and he went on to express a concern that the commission's proposals might permit an aggressive faculty to go too far too fast. That this was not an unwarranted concern is suggested by the opinion of a young faculty member that the commission did not go far enough in its recommendations. He stated that younger faculty members felt the commission's recommendations did provide the basis for further changes and that because of this, they supported the commission's proposals rather than initiating a fight over the failure (as they saw it) to go far enough. Given these two views, it may be concluded that the commission managed, overall, to find the very elusive middle ground between the perceived interests of the older and younger generation on the faculty.

Both in terms of Swarthmore itself and in terms of other institutions, significant changes took place in a remarkably unruffled atmosphere. There is no reason to believe, however, that Swarthmore has now caught up with the rapidly changing world of higher education. Further changes will surely come.

COMMENTARY   In my judgment the Swarthmore study was notably successful— its success more complete than that of any other institution included in this study. There are several apparent reasons for this success.

The first and probably most prominent reason for the success is the nature of Swarthmore itself. As a small, relatively wealthy, essentially single-purpose institution, it has both an élan and an identity which are well understood and shared by all its members. Swarthmore is a close approximation of—to use that badly overworked phrase—an educational community. [3] Furthermore, Swarthmore has for many, many years been an absolutely first-class institution, and without any arrogance Swarthmore knows this. As is so often true, those who are quite secure in their present position are those who can change most readily. The relative success of the Swarthmore self-study is undoubtedly one indication of why Swarthmore holds such an eminent position in the collegiate world.

A second reason for the success of the Swarthmore self-study lies in the widespread acceptance, from the very beginning, of the idea that such a study was needed. A substantial majority of the faculty, administration, and students felt the need for some changes before the commission began its work. To be sure, there were those who sought modest changes and those who sought radical changes and some, no doubt, who wished for the form of change without its substance. Nevertheless, the idea of change was widely accepted and was never seen as something being imposed

[3] The existence of such a community seems to be borne out by the apparent readiness of everyone—especially the faculty—to drop everything else to become involved in Super Week and the Danforth Groups. Such response is not typical in most institutions when decisions are to be made, let alone when the discussions are specifically not intended to result in action.

from the top down. Furthermore, by involving everyone as much as possible in its work, the commission tended to ensure that the readiness for change was kept alive. The fact that the general tenor of the commission's recommendations came as a great surprise to no one was surely helpful in achieving general acceptance.

A third essential element in Swarthmore's success was the leadership of President Smith. His sense of timing in inaugurating the study was impeccable. One of the signers of one of the letters asking President Smith to initiate a study suggested that much of the success resulted from the fact that the president moved so very promptly upon receipt of the letters—"really a breathtaking burst of decision-making power." The president's quick acceptance of the idea of Super Week and his firm control of the long and difficult process of faculty consideration stand out as major contributions to the success of the study. That President Smith was able to push everything through to a conclusion without apparently having aroused any resentment for "dictatorial tactics," "authoritarianism," or the like is, I take it, evidence of real leadership. Indeed, all faculty members and students at Swarthmore with whom I talked had nothing but praise for the president's handling of the whole affair.

Finally, and this is no doubt largely another manifestation of President Smith's administrative strength, was the recognition that the job of considering over 150 recommendations which affected virtually every aspect of the college was not treated casually. Plans for the Danforth Groups and for formal consideration were carefully made. During the spring, Dean Cobbs and the steering committee and the commission members devoted a tremendous amount of attention to ensuring that the job was kept moving—that it was not bogged down in trivia or smothered in verbosity, both of which so often characterize the process of academic debate. Careful planning and follow-up—neither of which is terribly common in the processes of academic policy making—were very much in evidence at Swarthmore.

# 6. Wesleyan University
## Study of Educational Policies and Programs

Wesleyan University has the enviable distinction of having the largest endowment per student of any college or university in the United States. It has also had a reputation—acquired especially since the end of World War II—for being innovative and experimental. For most of its history, Wesleyan, in spite of the university label, was basically an undergraduate liberal arts college. In very recent times, Wesleyan has inaugurated five Ph.D. programs, although most of its approximately 250 graduate students were enrolled in master's degree programs. Wesleyan enrolls about 1,400 undergraduate students (all men) and has recently been very active in recruiting black students. In 1969, some 10 percent of the members of the student body were black or were from other "disadvantaged" minority groups. The remainder of the Wesleyan undergraduates are very carefully selected and come from throughout the country. The Wesleyan faculty numbers about 250, and average faculty salaries are among the highest in the country.

Wesleyan has no professional schools or colleges. There are three undergraduate colleges—letters, social studies, and quantitative studies—which have very experimental programs, and there is an honors college which provides an opportunity for students to elect independent study for honors. The colleges, however, are basically teaching rather than administrative units, and the governance of the university rests formally with the university faculty. The Wesleyan faculty organization involves a separate senior faculty and junior faculty, the former including all tenured professors. These groups meet separately and also jointly. The Educational Policy Committee conducts much of the faculty business concerning curriculum and related matters and includes members of both the senior and the junior faculty. In large measure, these arrangements merely institutionalize the power of seniority which characterizes most faculties, but given the small size of the Wesleyan faculty, the effect of these arrangements has been concentration of power in the hands of a relatively small senior group. This has resulted in some alienation of junior people.

The Wesleyan study began early in 1967, and its recommendations and conclusions had been largely disposed of in one way or another by the end of 1968. The provost's office has been charged with the implementation of recommendations which were accepted. The study differs from the others reviewed in this report in two significant ways. Perhaps the most important difference is that it was done neither by a committee nor by an individual. Formal committees, informal groups, individuals, and a staff director were all involved. The process of the study has been not inappropriately described by President Etherington as a "floating crap game."

The second difference between the Wesleyan study and most of the others described here is that it was less concerned with changes in curriculum and academic procedures and much more involved with major structural changes in the university. The questions of coeducation and changes in, or elimination of, the Center for Advanced Studies[1] are representative of the kinds of issues with which the study was concerned.

**ORIGIN OF THE STUDY**  The Wesleyan study was intended primarily to provide the basic framework for the administration of a new president. Early in 1967, Edwin Etherington, then president of the American Stock Exchange, was elected by the Wesleyan trustees to succeed, on July 1, 1967, Victor Butterfield, who had been Wesleyan's president since 1942. President Butterfield had been responsible for a great many innovations and changes during his tenure at Wesleyan, but there seems to be general agreement that as he approached retirement, a number of unresolved issues began to accumulate. Furthermore, the many innovations of the Butterfield era were not particularly coordinated, and there was a widespread sense of fragmentation. Both of these conditions had resulted in some feel-

---

[1] The Center for Advanced Studies permitted distinguished scholars to go to Wesleyan and work in very desirable conditions for varying periods of time. In spite of the original intentions that the fellows of the center would be active participants in the life of the university, the center had become essentially a research center.

ings of frustration among faculty members. President-elect Etherington felt that a major study of educational programs and policies would identify the problems with which he would have to deal when he assumed office. He also hoped that such a study would serve to involve the entire community in working with him on these problems. Finally, such a study would buy some time for the new president, since action on controversial matters could be deferred, pending completion of the study. For example, the Wesleyan faculty had nearly unanimously endorsed an earlier report calling for the admission of women. Students, too, were heartily in favor of admitting women, but a majority of the trustees were opposed to such a move. Clearly, President Etherington needed time to work out such an issue.[2] Similarly, the trustees were anxious to have the university become much more involved in attempting to solve some of the problems of the community, a desire which was potentially, at least, in conflict with the more inward-looking academic interests of the faculty.

For all these reasons—to identify problems, involve the entire community, and buy some time—President-elect Etherington, almost immediately after his election, asked Provost Robert Rosenbaum to draw up a charge for a study of educational policies and programs and get it under way. Both because it was a natural accompaniment to the beginning of a new presidency and because there was a degree of restlessness among the faculty arising from the fragmentation and the relative lack of movement during the immediately preceding year or so, announcement of the study appears to have been received with widespread enthusiasm, though there was no widespread prior demand for such a study.

**CONDUCT OF THE STUDY** In January, 1967, Provost Rosenbaum asked three senior faculty members—one from each of the divisions of the faculty—to meet with him and draw up a charge for the study. Each of the faculty members was well known and generally respected, and their potential political positions were an important consideration in their selection. At the same time, John Maguire, an associate professor

[2] Wesleyan had been coeducational in its early years, but had banished women in the 1890s. Some disgruntled alumnae at once began a campaign to replace the opportunity for higher education for women, and the establishment, in 1911, of Connecticut College for Women resulted. Such are the changes in our wisdom about these matters that in the mid-1960s, the two institutions began exchanges of students, and each is moving to become fully coeducational. Perhaps another 50 years will reveal whether our grandparents or we knew best.

of religion, was given an 18-month, full-time assignment as staff director for the study.

In about a month this group issued a paper which identified the major issues with which the study would be concerned. These issues were presented to the faculty in a short working paper. This paper suggested that "Perhaps the most fundamental questions of focus and purpose concern the degree to which the university is to commit its resources and energy to scholarship and the life of the mind, or to outward-looking programs geared directly to serving the practical needs of other institutions (e.g. government, the schools, industry, etc.)" (Wes., 1). The paper then delineated several policy choices which needed to be made once the major direction was established. These included types of programs and facilities, faculty, students, university administration, and cooperation with other institutions.

When this paper was prepared and released in April, the steering group proceeded to begin various studies of specific issues which included outsiders. Many faculty members were involved in individual studies on, for example, faculty recruiting and faculty professional activities. As this work got under way, the provost and the staff director concluded that the summer would be a crucial period, and a summer working group made up of six faculty members, three students, and various outsiders was organized. The faculty and students were to work full time, and the outsiders were to be brought on campus as required. Late in the spring, the provost held a lengthy series of evening meetings to which the members of all departments were invited. By the end of the spring semester in 1967 the study was well under way, and most faculty members were involved in it in some fashion.

The Summer Working Group was administered largely by the provost. There was criticism of the personnel of the group both in terms of who was on it and in terms of who was not. There was no intention by the provost that every area of the faculty should be represented, but those areas not represented felt that the group should have been representative. The Summer Working Group organized itself into two- or three-member panels to be concerned with specific topics. Everyone was a member of six or seven of these panels, and twice a week the entire group had plenary meetings for half a day. By the end of the summer, these groups had developed analyses and some recommendations on 29 topics. At this point it was necessary to decide how to handle this mass of material.

In September, Professor Maguire became, in effect, the executive director of the study and began the task of organizing and disseminating the results of all the activities of the spring and summer. He consolidated the 29 topics into 10 major areas and discussed these in a series of 13 working papers which appeared roughly every two weeks between October and the end of January. The working papers discussed—sometimes in two or more installments—the admission of women, advanced learning, library facilities, undergraduate curriculum, academic reorganization, the Center for Advanced Studies, teacher education, cooperation with other institutions, student activities, and admissions. The papers did not include specific proposals for action, but for the most part they gave a statement of the problems, listed options available, discussed pros and cons, and proposed next steps for action.

These papers were printed as supplements in the *Argus,* the campus newspaper, generally consisting of three to four tabloid-sized pages of newsprint. They were widely discussed in general open meetings, in departmental and divisional meetings, and in all sorts of informal groups, and they gave rise to a great deal of letter writing. The flood of paper appears to have overwhelmed the Wesleyan faculty, and during the late fall and winter a generally unfavorable reaction to the process set in.

Opinions and recollections of what happened at Wesleyan during the winter vary, but there seems to be a consensus that everyone was fed up, irritated, and rather dismayed by the whole process. The statement of one faculty member sums up the feeling of many: "You began to feel that you were doing nothing but reading reports and being pushed into many problems that really didn't concern you." Not all faculty members had quite this reaction, for as one observed, "Most of the SEPP reports remained unread." Another widely shared view was that there was a great deal of talk but very little action. No decisions were being made, and new issues were constantly being introduced. As a result of these feelings, many people began to look for more sinister reasons. The way the study was being done permitted many to feel that the faculty was being "circumvented by faceless men." Because of President Etherington's previous connections with Wall Street, there were mutterings that he was the "master of the big power play." Professor Maguire came in for considerable criticism, partly, no doubt, because he was the one person whom everyone could associate with the study. Also, because of the great haste with which the working papers were prepared, there were a number of lapses in style and clarity which gave rise to much criticism. Junior faculty members and students appear not to have identified with the study and its objectives from the beginning, so their disenchantment simply increased. Among the student group, it was apparently an article of faith that the faculty members and students involved in the summer group had been picked to do the administration's bidding. In short, irritation about the study and uncertainty about where it was leading were widespread.

At this point, two things happened. Sensing the general malaise over both the progress and the process of the study, the president and the provost turned over all proposals concerning curriculum which had been made in the working papers to the regular Educational Policy Committee of the faculty. While this involved more group meetings, hearings, and impassioned oratory, it did lead to some actions on the part of the faculty. Principal among these were the elimination of all university curriculum requirements and the institution of a comprehensive academic advising system. Wesleyan had previously had a modest distribution requirement, a foreign language requirement, and an English requirement for all students. Except for the requirements of a major department or one of the colleges, the Wesleyan student now designs his own program. He is one of eight students assigned to a faculty adviser, and the advising program has a designated coordinator. A serious attempt is being made to ensure that the absence of stated requirements does not leave some students simply floundering.

It was also established that any faculty member could offer his courses on a pass-fail basis. The elimination of requirements was extremely controversial, and opinion was narrowly divided. It was suggested to me that the proposal was passed by the faculty only after a "job-protection" clause had been written in to relieve the fears of those departments which were heavily involved in teaching required courses.

The second thing that happened in the spring of 1968 was that the trustees decided to begin the admission of undergraduate women and to change substantially the Center for Advanced Studies. Since these two decisions were extremely popular with the faculty, the air was cleared considerably, and a feeling of progress was restored. There is no evidence that students were concerned about the Center for Advanced Studies, but not surprisingly, they led the rejoicing over the admission of women.

In May of 1968, a summary report containing a number of recommendations and analyses from previously circulated documents was prepared. In a full faculty meeting, President Etherington discussed this summary report and explained actions taken or to be taken. A short time later, he held a second meeting given over to answering faculty questions about the summary report. This final report, of course, was as much a historical record as anything else because, as explained above, many decisions to do or not to do various things were made as the study went along.

**ACHIEVE-MENTS** Since the Wesleyan study did not follow the usual pattern of presenting a long or short series of recommendations to decision-making bodies for action, it is not possible to make a summary statement of its achievements. Certain specific results can be identified. Women undergraduates are to be admitted. The Center for Advanced Studies has been replaced by a university Center for the Humanities, whose fellows will be members of the faculty—thereby avoiding isolation of the former center from the mainstream of the university. University curriculum requirements were abolished, and a more effective advising system was installed. An Institute for Public Affairs, which will provide a focus for Wesleyan's work in the outside community, is to be started. A guarded decision to proceed with the establishment of more Ph.D. programs and a recognition of the need to expand the library resulted. A proposal to have separate deans for each of the three divisions of the faculty was put aside after much consideration.

There appears to be general agreement with the statement of one faculty member that "SEPP was a failure in terms of its original purpose to get general agreement on a sort of master model for the university." The original prospectus for the study focused on a profound and contemporary question: Should the university "commit its resources and energy to scholarship and the life of the mind, or to outward-looking programs geared directly to serving the practical needs of other institutions?" (Wes., 1). The study never achieved a real confrontation with this issue, although it is possible that it was decided without ever being faced. Certainly the study indicated a rather broad consensus among the faculty that Wesleyan should move further into graduate study and research. This surely represents a reaffirmation of "scholarship and the life of the mind."

Beyond this, it was generally agreed that the study turned up a great deal of information about the strengths and weaknesses of Wesleyan and involved a great many people in developing plans and institutions for change.

COMMENTARY It is difficult to assess the Wesleyan study—especially within the frame of reference provided by most of the other studies. The Wesleyan curriculum was relatively open and experimental— many interdisciplinary courses and programs were in existence before the study began. There was virtually no teaching by other than regular faculty members, and large, impersonal classes were not at all common. In short, Wesleyan did not face certain of the problems dealt with in most of the other studies.

As already observed, the study did not achieve one of its principal purposes, which was to provide a master model for the university. However, it did buy some time for a new president, and it did involve very many people in a penetrating look at the university. As one faculty member, not particularly a supporter of the study, put it, "Everyone—senior faculty, junior faculty, and students— had a chance to put in his nickel's worth."

The study did contribute to the resolution of certain major issues —coeducation, for example—and certain changes in curriculum resulted from it. What is not clear is that these specific achievements required the major upheaval of the study.

The achievements of the study did not come without a price, however. Wesleyan's "winter of discontent" was perhaps made summer by the imminent arrival of women, but one has the distinct impression that the discontent was severe and has left some scars. That the process of the study involved a great many people is undoubtedly good, but the experience seems to suggest that in such situations people need some readily identifiable person or group who can be held responsible for all that has been done or overlooked. Wesleyan was fortunate that very widespread respect for Provost Rosenbaum provided a degree of needed confidence in the long-run outcome of the study.

In short, one has the feeling that the crap game floated just a bit too much. Visiting Wesleyan a few months after the study was ostensibly finished, one sensed a feeling of exhaustion rather than of euphoria. One faculty member stated, "We must have ten years of tranquility." In these days in academia, one does not need to have been through a year-and-a-half-long self-study to feel that way, of course. Nonetheless, one wonders whether the accomplishments of the Wesleyan study might not have been brought about with somewhat less upset.

# 7. Michigan State University

## Improving Undergraduate Education

Michigan State, the "pioneer land-grant institution," is one of the largest American universities, with, in 1969, over 40,000 students. Over 20,000 of these reside in university dormitories on its huge campus. Until the years following World War II, the university was a characteristic land-grant college. Its agriculture departments are still among the nation's largest and most prominent, but in recent years the university has made a move toward the select university world of scholarship, graduate work, National Merit Scholars, and the like. For 27 years, until early 1969, it had been under the leadership of President John Hannah, and as one faculty member put it, "Michigan State is Hannah."

In 1969, the tenured faculty of the university numbered about 2,200. Educational functions were carried on through 16 colleges, including three independent undergraduate liberal arts colleges and an honors college, as well as the more traditional specialized colleges. The undergraduate liberal arts colleges were established primarily as an attempt to offset some of the effects of huge size. For the same reason, the university had established a number of "living-learning" units, which combined residence facilities with classrooms, faculty offices, and libraries. These latter are not academic units in the strict sense, as the liberal arts colleges are.

University government is based on a senate, which includes all tenured faculty members. The locus of government is in the Academic Council, which includes deans of the colleges, members of the central administration, chairmen of council committees, and elected representatives of the colleges. In 1969, there were two student members of the Academic Council, and most of the standing committees of the council had one graduate student and one undergraduate student as members. Major actions of the Academic Council are subject to approval by the senate, but as a practical matter the Academic Council has basic authority over matters of curriculum, academic standards, and the like.

The Committee on Undergraduate Education was appointed by President Hannah in February, 1967, although the decision to create such a committee had been made and selection of its membership had begun during the summer of 1966. The committee completed its work during the spring and summer of 1967 and issued its report in October, 1967. Shortly afterward, an assistant provost for undergraduate education was appointed and given the task of coordinating the consideration and implementation of the report's recommendations. Prior to this appointment, certain of the committee's recommendations relating to general education had been introduced into the Academic Council and precipitated a rather bitter and lengthy debate. When this ended, the atmosphere was no longer particularly conducive to further consideration of committee recommendations. The assistant provost directed most of his efforts toward working through individual departments to bring about the changes recommended by the committee. These efforts resulted in some changes, but in February, 1969, the assistant provost left the university and was not immediately replaced. The drive toward implementation of the report's recommendations, which his efforts represented, was considerably diminished. More or less simultaneously President Hannah left to join the national government, and most of those who might have provided leadership for implementation were drawn into the issues surrounding selection of his successor. Consequently, by the spring of 1969 formal efforts to implement the changes proposed by the committee had been largely stalled. Relatively few of its important recommendations had been acted upon, and there seemed little likelihood that they would be.

ORIGIN OF THE STUDY     The idea of undertaking a fairly wide-ranging study of undergraduate education originated largely at the administrative level and more particularly within the office of the provost. The provost's staff, in a series of discussions about the problems and priorities of the university, concluded that undergraduate education needed attention more than any other aspect of the university's operation. Once this conclusion had been reached, it was almost automatic that a "blue-ribbon" university-wide committee would be created to carry out the task of focusing attention on the subject. The use of such committees is a traditional way of dealing with major problems at Michigan State.

There is no indication that the undertaking of such a study was specifically in response to widespread demand or concern on the part of faculty members or students. Several faculty members indicated to me that some were concerned about the nature of undergraduate education on the campus, but the concern appears not to have been very widespread and certainly had no particular focus. On the other hand, in spite of its huge size and a rather rapid move into big-time graduate work, Michigan State under President Hannah had retained a degree of concern with undergraduate education which is somewhat unusual in such an institution.

The history of Michigan State in the years just prior to the formation of the Committee on Undergraduate Education had involved a great deal of university-wide attention to change and to undergraduate education. In 1958, the university's tremendous growth was well under way. It had joined the Big Ten, which involved a shift away from its "aggie school" tradition. Related to both of these was rather large-scale recruiting of many professionally oriented faculty members who were much more devoted to "excellence" than to "state." All these pressures resulted in the convening of a Committee on the Future, which prepared a blueprint for development of the university. Among other things, this led to the establishment of the living-learning units beginning in 1961 and of the residential colleges beginning in 1965. In 1964, with the help of a matching Ford Foundation grant, an Educational Development Program was established. Part of the provost's office, this program is "devoted to the development and implementation of a set of educational principles and procedures . . . which will be developed and approved by the general faculty and which will preserve and improve undergraduate education." This program has been responsible for the gathering of much important information, for a number of special studies, and for developments in curriculum and instruction. In short, there had been a fairly continuous process of university-wide examination of various matters of educational policy and a number of specific developments related to undergraduate education. As one faculty member put it, "From 1959 on, Hannah never let anything settle." Thus, while there was no apparent demand for such a study, neither was a stir created when Provost Neville spoke about the problem of undergraduate education before the senate and asked for presidential appointment of a committee to study undergraduate education. In 1966, such investigations were almost the order of the day at Michigan State.

SELECTION
OF THE
COMMITTEE The committee members were chosen by the provost—some of them directly, and some on the recommendation of college deans, in accord with Michigan State practice for choosing such a committee.

Provost Howard R. Neville pointed out that there was no alternative to having a representative of each of Michigan State's six basic undergraduate colleges on the committee. Beyond this constraint, he was guided by a number of factors in selecting members, one of which was the necessity of looking ahead to the time when the committee would have its report and ask the question, "Now that we've got a report, whom do we wish had written it?" A second consideration was to have as chairman a faculty member who was absolutely "clean" in terms of his position in the faculty, who was a respected scholar, and who was an experienced committeeman. Finally, Provost Neville felt it necessary to have a representative from the honors college because he anticipated that a number of issues involving it would loom large in committee deliberations. The chairman and the member from the honors college were chosen directly by the provost. One other member, Prof. Harry H. Kimber, was chosen because of his long involvement with the development of University College, which had for some time been the focus of some controversy. He had also served on many important university committees. Beyond these, the provost selected members from among the nominees of the undergraduate colleges on the basis of their apparent ability to work with the others, their articulateness and forcefulness, and the extent to which they were representative of their peers. As might be expected in such a large university, some of the nominees were not known to the provost before he talked with them about service on the committee.

Finally, Provost Neville put himself on the committee. His principal reason for doing so, apparently, was to indicate to the university community that the work of the committee was of first-rank importance. (In some institutions such a move would have immediately resulted in the committee's being seen as a "tool of the administration." There is no indication that this was a common reaction at Michigan State.)

**TABLE 5** *Membership of the Committee on Undergraduate Education, Michigan State University*

| Name and rank | Field | Age group* | Years at MSU | Degrees from MSU |
|---|---|---|---|---|
| Arthur E. Adams, professor | History | 50–57 | 16 | None |
| James L. Dye, professor | Chemistry | 34–41 | 14 | None |
| James D. Edwards, professor | Accounting | 34–41 | 16 | None |
| John X. Jamrich, professor | Education | 42–49 | N.A. | None |
| Harry H. Kimber, professor | Religion | Over 58 | 37 | None |
| Lester Manderscheid, associate professor | Agricultural economics | 34–41 | 11 | None |
| James B. McKee, professor | Sociology | 42–49 | 8 | None |
| Howard R. Neville, provost | Sociology | 42–49 | 13 | Ph.D. |
| Willard Warrington, professor | Evaluation services | 42–49 | 15 | None |
| John Wilson, assistant professor | English Honors Col. | 34–41 | 4 | A.B., Ph.D. |
| John Zimmer, professor | Natural science | 50–57 | 34 | M.A. |

*Ages and years at the institution are given as of the time the committee was first convened.

According to Provost Neville, no one thought of having any persons from outside the university on the committee, nor was the matter of student membership given serious consideration while the committee was being formed.

Announcement of the membership of the committee was not greeted with wild enthusiasm. Some members were well known and widely respected; some were well known and rather more controversial. Several were virtually unknown in the university at large, not surprising in an institution with over 2,000 faculty members. It is perhaps also not surprising that an indeterminate but significant number of faculty members were unaware of the committee's existence.

CONDUCT OF THE STUDY

It appears that the committee rather quickly overcame the lack of enthusiasm which greeted its creation. As one faculty member put it, "The committee came in quietly, but the quality of its performance while at work, the questions it asked, and the manner of its procedures were all very impressive to many faculty members."

The committee worked under a very broad charge from President Hannah. Except for the specific focus on undergraduate education, the committee could not, in President Hannah's words, "help being concerned with curriculum, teaching, advising, and the academic climate." This seems a clear direction to be very broad, limited only by the president's reference to "allegiance to the best of our traditions." He went on to suggest that "Michigan State University is a land-grant, state-supported institution which has found great validity in professional-vocational education firmly based on liberal-general education for all students."

When the formation of the committee was announced, there was some demand for student membership. This demand was met by inviting students to set up an essentially parallel group which would carry on some of its own investigations and assist the faculty committee in the latter's work. The student group ran a number of hearings on specific issues and gathered a great deal of data which the committee used. This work, along with full publicity given by the Michigan State *News,* the student newspaper, was of great assistance to the committee. Deans and other key people in the university presented papers on their particular problems, and several open hearings were held on specific topics. A rather comprehensive questionnaire was sent to 1,394 faculty members (483 completed questionnaires were returned to the committee). The committee did not make use of consultants or experts from outside the university. In general, it may be said that the work of the committee was highly visible to the university community throughout its life.

Within the committee, the chairman "ran a tight ship," as one member put it. Early meetings were taken up largely with having each member identify the problems which particularly concerned him and by having Provost Neville give background material to the committee. The chairman kept the committee out of debates on educational philosophy because of his conviction that they would be nonproductive.

With one exception, the committee's report appears to represent a genuine consensus of members' views. After full discussion of the various issues, each member was assigned a specific topic about which to prepare a draft. Several of these drafts were substantially rewritten by the chairman or the executive secretary, and thus the final report probably bears the particular stamp of these two, although it was clearly quite acceptable to the whole group.

The one exception to the broad consensus was the matter of University College.[1] On this point, all members agreed that the report was a narrow compromise between sharply opposing views. Some members felt that University College should be abolished, and others that it should be retained and strengthened. The committee's final recommendation was essentially a halfway compromise. Substitutions would be permitted for the American thought and letters sequence and for the sequence which was in the same area as the student's major. In effect, the amount of time spent taking University College courses could be cut in half if the student wished to.

During the winter term in 1967, the committee met three mornings a week, and during the spring term meetings were held daily. Drafting of the report was completed during the summer of 1967, and it was distributed to the faculty and (through the campus newspaper) to students in the early fall. All committee members expressed a feeling that the time allotted to them was too short and too compressed. From a luncheon meeting with most of the committee members, I got the impression of a general feeling that if there had been somewhat more leisurely deliberation, the report would have been improved.

**SUMMARY OF THE RECOMMENDATIONS** *Improving Undergraduate Education* was broad in its scope. Discussions of, and recommendations about, admissions policy, teaching, curriculum, advising, academic climate, and administration were included. A number of recommendations called for formal legislation by the faculty; some were addressed to the academic departments; many called for administrative action. Many recommendations simply called for increased attention to processes and attitudes which had been proposed by earlier committees. Overall, the impact of the report to a reader who is not a member of the university is that of exhortation to the faculty to consider changes and invitation to the administration to exercise leadership in bringing about change.

[1] University College at Michigan State is essentially a general-education division in which all entering freshmen are enrolled. The college has four departments: American thought and letters, the natural sciences, social science, and the humanities. Each of these departments endeavors to give general education courses in the "Harvard Redbook" sense and not in the survey-course sense. At the time the study began, all freshmen were normally required to enroll in the University College sequences in American thought and letters and the natural sciences. In the sophomore year, the sequences in social science and the humanities were normally required.

Many of the recommendations concern technical matters relating specifically to Michigan State, but the essence of the more general recommendations is given below.

**Admissions** The committee had two principal concerns with admissions. The first was to check the unrestrained growth, which had seen the university's enrollment jump from 19,000 in 1959 to 38,000 in 1967. The committee's expressed concern was with the "internal imbalances and over-extension" which resulted from the rapid growth. Neither a reduction in size nor a specific ceiling on future growth was mentioned, although the report's rhetoric rather clearly implies a feeling that the university had been allowed to become too large.

The committee's second concern was to avoid what they saw as "a drift toward a totally middle-class, Middle Western student body." To achieve an undergraduate community "reflecting the diversity of social classes and values found in the larger society" and to deal with the issue of size, the committee recommended that the admissions function be placed in the office of the provost and that a faculty Standing Committee on Admissions be established. This committee would be given a major responsibility for the formulation of admissions policy.

**Teaching** The committee's report includes a rather extensive discussion of teaching which implies—and occasionally specifically states—that it is not always of very high quality. Enormous size, increased attention to graduate and research programs, "indiscriminate" use of graduate students as teachers, and inadequate evaluation of teachers were all cited by the committee as specific problems.

Most of the recommendations relating to these problems involve a good deal of exhortation—not surprising, given the nature of the problem. Each department was urged to establish a Committee on Teaching, and these committees were asked to work with one another and with the provost for the improvement of teaching. Provision for small classes (essentially, budgetary provision) and for more adequate instructional facilities was proposed. Attempts to recruit the most able graduate students as teaching assistants and to use them as assistants rather than as substitute professors were proposed, as were awards to teaching assistants for excellence in teaching.

The report urged greater use of student evaluations of courses and teaching. (Actually, the recommendation was a reaffirmation of earlier faculty legislation.) Furnishing these evaluations to department chairmen and beyond would not be required, although faculty members were "encouraged to have these summary reports sent to their department chairmen so that the results can be involved in decisions pertaining to them."

**Academic Climate** The committee was rather strong in its indictment of many faculty members for a failure to accept responsibility for the overall climate of the university, for the "values which it honors." Much the same charges were leveled against the nonacademic staff with whom students are most frequently in contact, such as dining hall and residence managers and business office and registrar personnel. In more specific terms, the committee's recommendations were directed toward further developing and strengthening the living-learning complexes which had been created at Michigan State. The committee's concern was that these become "genuine inter-collegiate units of instruction and residence." Specific recommendations were intended to bring more instruction into these units in a planned and coordinated way and to improve the style and quality of residential life. The final recommendation concerning climate was for the early construction of a fine arts center, including a concert hall.

**General Education** A principal recommendation in the area of general education was referred to above—the substitution of elective courses for two of the University College general education sequences. The perennial problem of writing skill was attacked through the perennial recommendation that more emphasis be given to it in the first-year course. Departments were urged to expand their offerings appropriate for nonmajors, and the development of integrative senior-level courses was urged. More consultation between the University College faculty and members of other university departments was called for.

**Other Curriculum Matters** The report suggested that some of the majors offered in the university did not belong in the university on the grounds that they lacked contact with basic disciplines or did "not continue to speak to social needs of high priority" and recommended that appropriate university committees review all majors to see whether they should be continued. Also recommended was a departmental and college review of all majors to determine those which were too highly prescribed or too loosely structured. It was also recommended that departments try to develop courses which were "conditioned neither by the usual credit offerings nor the usual time of one of our present offerings." The committee also made a number of technical proposals intended to make possible a closer identification of the student with his major department.

**Advising**  The committee reviewed the usual difficulties with academic advising: too few advisers, too much clerical work, too little faculty interest, and too little time for the necessary relationships to develop. To overcome some of these problems, the establishment of college advising centers with "professional" advisers was proposed. These would be concerned with students primarily during their first two years. The departments were asked to focus their efforts on advising during the junior and senior years.

**Special Programs**  The report proposed strengthening the honors college, which at Michigan State was basically a structural device that permitted more able students to pursue their own courses of study. Especially, the committee recommended that the basis for admission into the honors college be broadened to include more than the high grade-point average, which had been the principal criterion.

In the case of the independent, degree-granting experimental colleges, the committee's recommendations were cautionary. At one level, the committee was concerned that the attempts to overcome the disadvantages of size and to permit educational experimentation generally would be limited to these colleges—that the same problems in the regular undergraduate colleges would be ignored. At another level, the committee was concerned with the evaluation of experimental proposals both before and after the fact. There is an implication that the colleges were perhaps too independent. To deal with both of these problems, the report proposed creation of a committee which would regularly consult with, and review the activities of, the colleges.

**Administration**  Perhaps the key proposal made by the committee was that for creation of the position of vice-provost for undergraduate education. This was intended to keep in balance the "centrifugal and centripetal forces within the university" so that the central administration would be able to "provide effectively for the interests of undergraduate education." Obeisance was made to departmental and collegiate autonomy, but it seems clear that the committee intended that there be a very powerful spokesman for undergraduate education at a high level in the central administration of the university.

Before completing its work, the committee deliberated at some length as to the disposition of the report. Some members argued that the committee's proposals should, where appropriate, be put in a form suitable for submission to the Academic Council. That is, with the submission of its report, the committee would initiate the process of consideration and action. Other members of the committee, including the chairman, felt that since the committee had been appointed by the president rather than being an elected faculty committee, it could and should report only to the president. Furthermore, it was argued that a relatively large committee could not draft legislation. Eventually it was decided to submit the report to the president with some informal recommendations as to what might be done with it.

Members of the committee subsequently agreed that momentum was lost as a result of this decision. There was a substantial time lag between distribution of the report and the beginning of formal consideration—a time lag which had some serious consequences. At the same time, one has the impression that no other decision could have been made. The tradition of faculty independence at Michigan State seems strong enough to have ensured an unfavorable reception of specific proposals from a presidential committee.

When the report came out, President Hannah issued a statement indicating his general support of its substance and asking for widespread discussion. At about the same time the central administration—more or less in accord with the committee's proposal —appointed an assistant provost for undergraduate education. Professor Wilson, who had been secretary of the committee, was appointed to the post and given the specific task of working on implementation. This action no doubt served as a signal to the university that the administration took the report seriously. It also ensured that there would be someone specifically concerned with the process of consideration and implementation of the report. At the same time, Professor Wilson was appointed assistant provost—not vice-provost, as the report had recommended—and it appears that his authority and responsibility fell rather short of those contemplated in the report. It was suggested to me that some of the college deans objected strongly to making this new post a really powerful one.

Before Provost Wilson was actually appointed, those parts of the report requiring legislation about curriculum and related matters were turned over to the steering committee of the Academic Council. This is the point at which the time lag between the submission of the report and the planning for its consideration had an important effect. The assistant provost was not involved in determining the order in which the proposals would be brought before the council, nor was he able to prepare the way for discussions. The general education proposals were put on the agenda first. The English department introduced counterproposals, and the battle between University College and the regular university departments —which the committee had been at great pains to resolve through compromise—was immediately joined. No overall discussion "in principle" of the ideas and proposals written in the report was ever undertaken, but the gut issue of departmental sovereignty and self-interest was immediately raised. Ultimately, the council did vote to permit substitution of either an English department composition course or waiver on the basis of examination for the previously required University College sequence in American thought and letters. Also, the student could substitute departmental courses for the previously required University College sequence in the field in which his major existed. In essence, the committee's recommendation to reduce by one-half the organized general education courses required was passed. However, the fight over these proposals was wide-ranging and bitter. One faculty member stated that the resulting division between University College and the College of Arts and Letters "will never be healed." Never is, of course, a long time, but it is clear that the fight did, in effect, make it impossible to consider in a serious way any of the committee's other curriculum recommendations.

The assistant provost turned his attention during the fall of 1968 to working with individual departments. As a result of his efforts, a number of departments set up committees on teaching and obtained some awards for excellence of teaching assistants. Some courses outside the traditional three-credit mold were introduced, and some departments, under Professor Wilson's prodding, began to review their majors. However, as noted above, Professor Wilson left the university in February, 1969, and was not replaced by May of 1969. More or less simultaneously President Hannah retired, and several top administrators were involved in the succession. In short, consideration of *Improving Undergraduate Education* was confined largely to consideration by the Academic Council of the general-education issue and to Professor Wilson's efforts to influence departments. As suggested earlier, many of the report's recommendations called for continuing and strengthening some ongoing activities, and while budgetary limitations generally precluded strengthening, these were kept on.

On the whole, it seems clear that the report's principal impact on the university came through the divisive fight about general education which it precipitated. No doubt it has had some effect on what departments do, but one member of the university stated that after Professor Wilson's departure, enthusiasm for change within the departments noticeably diminished.

COMMENTARY   In the sense that it was an effort to redirect, strengthen, and devote more attention and resources to undergraduate education at Michigan State, *Improving Undergraduate Education* had limited success. It no doubt stimulated many individuals and small groups to think about the problems of undergraduate education, but there is little evidence that specific and concrete changes resulted in the year and a half following its publication.

An important reason for this lack of success is implicit in the nature of Michigan State itself. It is questionable whether any institution with 40,000 students, 2,200 tenured faculty members, 16 colleges, and 70 departments teaching undergraduates can be brought to move, as an institution, in even moderately different directions. At least, it is unlikely to be moved without very forceful—perhaps authoritarian—leadership.

It seems clear that the Committee on Undergraduate Education understood this and made as its central recommendation the appointment of a highly placed, powerful tsar (my word, not the committee's) to direct most of the other changes it proposed. What the committee had in mind is indicated by the following introduction to its discussion of administration:

The administration of a university is charged with a threefold function. First, it is the responsibility of the administrator, in all of his manifestations from assistant department chairman to the President, to direct the affairs of the institution, by the arts of persuasion as well as by the judicious exercise of authority, to the end that it accomplishes those purposes for which it exists and is supported by society. Secondly, because there may exist, within the bounds of loyalty to the general purpose of the institution, competing forces among the several parts of which it is composed, it is the function of the administrator to make decisions of priority, to employ in some cases encouragement and in others restraint, so as to weld together in a creative manner the tensions which inevitably arise. The third obligation which rests upon administration has a dual aspect: on the one hand, it is charged with oversight of the functioning of the various parts of the institution in order to insure that each is performing its assigned functions with maximum efficiency within the resources which are made available to it; on the other hand, it must manage to obtain adequate resources for the carrying out of the university's total role in society, and this without sacrifice of integrity or surrender of principle.

Ultimately, the university administration chose not to make such an appointment, at least not with the status and power which the committee suggested. Thus there was very little force behind the many recommendations addressed to colleges, departments, and individuals. While he was on the job, Professor Wilson's accomplishments were not negligible, but with his departure, it seems clear that truly fundamental change was not involved.

A second, lesser problem is related to timing. The time lag which resulted from the lack of prior plans for dealing with the report surely denied whatever advantage came from forward momentum. It seems that the activities of the committee engendered a great deal of interest and enthusiasm—and, no doubt, anxiety too—but when the report, in effect, lay on the table for some time before action was taken, much of this was lost.

*Improving Undergraduate Education* probably also illustrates the limited effectiveness of rhetoric and passion alone. Much of the text is passionate. It calls a spade a spade and clearly tries to communicate a spirit of needed change. As much as any other of the reports reviewed in this study, it is a call to arms. Perhaps with more forceful leadership and direction of the process of discussion and action, the rhetoric might have helped carry the day. Without these, it seems to have had little effect.

# 8. Duke University
## Varieties of Learning Experience

Duke is the only private university in the South which has national stature. Long regarded as something of a country club catering to the sons and daughters of upper-middle-class Southerners, Duke has lately joined the meritocracy of high SAT scores, a national student body, and a ranking in the Cartter report.

Duke officially describes itself as related to the Methodist Church, although for most practical purposes it is nonsectarian. Nevertheless, the Methodist Church retains a strong interest in the university, which grew out of Trinity College, a Methodist institution.

In addition to undergraduate work in arts and sciences, engineering, and nursing, the university offers graduate instruction in arts and sciences, divinity, forestry, law, and medicine. Overall, the university enrolled about 7,800 students in 1968 and had about 900 faculty members. Some 3,000 of the students are graduate students, and perhaps half of the faculty is engaged primarily in graduate and professional instruction. About two-thirds of the undergraduates are men. All undergraduates in arts and sciences are enrolled in Trinity College (men) or in Women's College. These are primarily administrative and residential units and do not have faculties associated with them. After earning a bachelor's degree, the vast majority of male Duke students continue academic work, primarily in professional schools such as business, law, and medicine.

The events described here are concerned entirely with undergraduate instruction in arts and sciences. Authority over curriculum and related matters rests with the Undergraduate Faculty Council of the faculty of arts and sciences. The Undergraduate Faculty Council has 120 members, including the chairman and director of undergraduate studies of each arts and science department. There are several *ex officio* members from the administration. The balance of the council is made up of members elected by individual departments, which have from one to three elected representatives, depending on their size. The dean of arts and sciences is the chairman of the council. As might be expected, a body of this size does most of its work through committees and subcommittees. Membership on these committees is by appointment by the dean on the recommendation of a committee on committees. Committee members need not be members of the Undergraduate Faculty Council.

The present study began in the spring of 1967, when the Subcommittee on Curriculum of the Committee on Instruction of the Undergraduate Faculty Council undertook an overall study of the Duke undergraduate curriculum. The committee issued a report in March, 1968, which included 11 recommendations. The Undergraduate Faculty Council considered the report during the balance of the spring semester, and with some modifications the recommendations were accepted prior to the end of the academic year 1968.

**ORIGIN OF THE STUDY** The Duke study evolved from a rather lengthy chain of circumstances. In 1959, the then-provost and the then-president of the university created a Long-range Planning Committee charged with investigating all aspects of university educational policy. This committee created a subcommittee on the undergraduate colleges to be concerned with such topics as curriculum, quality of teaching, admissions, and residential life. In 1960, this subcommittee presented to the Undergraduate Faculty Council a series of proposals for a substantial lessening of curriculum requirements. The Undergraduate Faculty Council considered these proposals over an 18-month period and eventually approved changes which made the requirements even more rigid than those which the subcommittee had recommended be relaxed.

During much of the period of consideration, Duke was in something of a ferment because both the president and the provost had been dismissed by the Board of Trustees. In what was a rather leaderless and uncertain situation, logrolling among the several departments began and got out of hand, with the result that a proposal to have fewer requirements actually produced more requirements. Also contributing to the result were circumstances that found most of the key members of the subcommittee responsible for the proposals to relax requirements away from the campus during the debates in the council, and so the proposals had little dedicated and informed support.

After 1962, some of those who had supported relaxation of requirements continued to work for this objective in conversations and meetings. There were also other pressures for change during this period. For example, one has the impression that many faculty members—including supporters of the final decisions in 1962— were somewhat chagrined by the rampant departmental self-interest which took over the debates in 1960–61. Even though they "won," they were not averse to a reconsideration. Another factor was an awareness that most of the institutions with which Duke considers itself competitive, such as those in the Ivy League, the Seven Sisters, and the more prestigious Big Ten universities, were substantially reducing general curriculum requirements in the mid-1960s. Since the Duke curriculum was considerably more restrictive than the curricula at many of these other institutions had been, even before the latter began to reduce requirements, it was clear that Duke was getting farther from current fashions in curriculum structure. For all these reasons, the question of restructuring the curriculum was not settled by the 1962 decision.

In the spring of 1966, the outgoing Subcommittee on Curriculum had written a rather strong indictment of the restrictive Duke curriculum. In the fall of that year, a number of strong supporters of curriculum liberalization, including members of the earlier Long-range Planning Committee, found themselves together in key positions on the Undergraduate Faculty Council.[1] These people, led by Assistant Dean Fred Jeorg, decided that it was a propitious time to move for change. They used the report of the previous committee as a basis for obtaining a grant from the Board of Higher Education of the Methodist Church to support a general study of the curriculum. Dean Jeorg and his associates felt that many aspects

---

[1] A sidelight on the nature of university government is revealed by this circumstance. Apparently, service on the Undergraduate Faculty Council was not widely sought after by senior faculty members, and so, in departmental elections, the assignments were often given to younger men. Thus, when a group of more senior people became determined to bring about change, they had much ready-made support from the many younger members of the council.

of educational policy other than curriculum should be studied, but made an essentially political decision that the time was more nearly ripe for curriculum revisions and that these might be delayed if many other changes were proposed at the same time. One member of the committee suggested that very few of the faculty members had any real interest in student residential life, for example, and that proposals to relate curriculum change to residential life, as some suggested, would have lessened the chances of success of the former. Furthermore, it was felt that if changes in the curriculum were made, they might then speed changes in other areas.[2]

In a certain sense, the decision to undertake the study grew out of previous actions which had resolved nothing. On the other hand, Dean Jeorg and faculty colleagues worked informally to keep the issue of reform alive and to prepare the way for a renewed effort to bring about change. Thus, while there was no widespread demand for change among Duke faculty members, they had been prepared for renewed consideration of curriculum and related matters.

**SELECTION OF THE COMMITTEE** Decisions about who would do the study appear to have evolved in much the same manner as the basic decision to have it done. No serious consideration was given to the appointment of an ad hoc committee outside the structure of the Undergraduate Faculty Council. However, it is regular practice at Duke for council committees to be staffed by persons who are not members of the council. Thus, while some of the status possibly connected with a special committee may have been lost, the actual group chosen to make the study was not unlike the ad hoc groups utilized elsewhere. That is, people were selected because of their interest in, and apparent qualifications for, the job.

Officially, members of the Subcommittee on Curriculum were appointed by the dean of arts and sciences upon recommendation of the Committee on Committees. Actually, committee membership was established largely by Dean Jeorg and the informal group which pushed for the study to be made. No particular attempt was made to obtain precise representation of all areas of the faculty. There

---

[2] Subsequently, a special committee on residential life was appointed and is considering such things as the creation of small, independent colleges which would combine living and study. The dean of Trinity College suggested that the curriculum changes already voted had given this new committee something very specific to work with.

**TABLE 6** *Membership of the Subcommittee on Curriculum, Duke University*

| Name and rank | Field | Age group* | Years at Duke | Degrees from Duke |
|---|---|---|---|---|
| *John Altrocchi, associate professor* | Psychology | 34–41 | 9 | None |
| *Hugh Hall, associate professor†* | Political science | 42–49 | 14 | None |
| *Frederick Joerg, professor‡* | Economics and business | 50–57 | 20 | None |
| *Robert Krueger, assistant professor* | English | Under 33 | 6 | None |
| *Harold Parker, professor* | History | Over 58 | 28 | None |
| *Bruce Wardropper, professor* | Romance languages | 42–49 | 7 | None |
| *Paul Welsh, professor* | Philosophy | Over 58 | 19 | None |
| *Donald Fluke, professor* | Zoology | 42–49 | 8 | None |

*Ages and years at the institution are given as of the time the committee was first convened.
†Associate dean, Trinity College, and dean of freshmen.
‡Assistant dean of arts and sciences.

was, for example, only one scientist (the chairman) among the eight members of the committee. All members, however, were known to be in favor of some change.

The most senior member of the committee had been a leader of the 1959 curriculum study under the Long-range Planning Committee. The staff director was a youngish assistant professor of English. All other committee members were in mid-career, and two were primarily administrators. (Most Duke administrators do some teaching.) Because of the grant from the Methodist Church it was possible for the staff director to spend full time on the study and for the other members to have some released time. The funds were also used to support traveling and to bring some consultants to the campus. No thought was given to having anyone from outside the university sit with the committee. A student nominated by the Associated Students of Duke University was designated as a student associate and participated fully in all the committee's deliberations. He did not, however, sign the report as a member of the committee.

The evidence I have indicates that the membership of the committee was widely accepted by the faculty. (The faculty of arts and sciences numbers about 450, and because Duke is a rather closely knit community, most members seem to know one another, by reputation if not personally.) Even some of those who were much at odds with the committee's recommendations agreed that the members were first-rate men.

**COMMITTEE OPERATION**  The committee was charged to make a careful study of the Duke curriculum as a whole and began its deliberations by discussing the basic philosophy of a curriculum, although there is no indication that it ever felt the need to produce a statement of philosophy. Basically, the committee reached its final positions by having each member draw up what he regarded as an ideal and "radical" curriculum. With apparently little disagreement, the committee quickly focused on three of these, which, though modified by discussion, became the basis for the final committee recommendations. Once the committee became reasonably certain of the directions in which it wished to move, it began discussions with each of the departments and among the faculty generally. Student-faculty advisory groups were set up to deal with specific topics, including such things as the quality of undergraduate instruction, the role of the creative arts, work-study programs, and the like. Reports of many of these advisory groups were included as appendixes to the committee's report, although many of them are peripheral to concerns reflected in the committee's recommendations. The committee also made a number of surveys of various student groups and of some recent alumni of the university. On the whole, it may be said that the committee worked very much in the open and that the general drift of its proposals was well known to most of the community before its final report was published.

**SUMMARY OF THE RECOMMENDATIONS**  As noted previously, the proposals at Duke were specifically related to curriculum, although the report contains, in appendixes, discussions of such matters as advising, quality of instruction, and the role of the performing arts. It was intended that some of these matters would be the subject of later proposals.

**Curriculum**  The Duke proposals had two overall objectives: to liberalize curriculum requirements which, for a contemporary, front-rank university, were remarkably restrictive, and partially to replace the traditional requirements of distribution of study over the areas of the curriculum with a distribution of study over a variety of "learning experiences."

The variety of learning experiences would come as follows: in each of the freshman and sophomore years students would be required to enroll in one course described as a seminar or in two courses described as preceptorials, discussion sections, or tutorials.[3] During the junior and senior years, each student would be required to take the equivalent of two courses as seminars or independent study, or to write a thesis.

The subject-matter distribution was not entirely eliminated. A student would be required to elect courses in each of the following: the social sciences, the natural sciences, and the humanities. He would take as many as the major department required in its division (subject to overall limits on major department requirements), four semester courses in a second division (of which at least two would be advanced courses), and two semester courses in the third division. The student was free to choose the individual courses needed to meet these requirements. The requirement for proficiency in English composition would be retained, but existing requirements in mathematics or logic and in a foreign language would be abandoned. The proposed requirements were considerably less restrictive than the 69 out of 124 semester hours—largely introductory-level courses—which Duke had been requiring.

In addition, the student would have to pass 12 semester courses at an advanced level, including those in his required concentration. The major departments were limited in the number of courses they could require: eight courses above the elementary level for the B.A. degree and ten for the B.S. The student was free to make further elections in his major field.

All the foregoing were included in what the committee called "Program I." In addition, the committee proposed adoption of a Program II, which was basically a way in which a student, upon the recommendation of a department, could design his own program without restriction by Program I requirements. A special committee would be created to supervise these independent programs and to recommend students for degrees.

The committee also proposed development of a Program III, under which specially designed curricula (the Tussman Program at

---

[3] In Duke's usage, a seminar is a course with about 12 students—not exceeding 15. A preceptorial is an additional and optional unit attached to a regular course and involves about 12 students. A discussion section (10 students) is also part of a course, but replaces lectures. A tutorial is a meeting of one to three students with a faculty member and is not a part of another course.

Berkeley was given as an illustration) could be developed and substituted for the regular Program I curriculum.

Finally, it was proposed that students, with the approval of an adviser and the faculty member involved, be freely permitted to do independent study. Along with these proposals, designed to permit greater student freedom, went a recommendation to reduce the normal student load from five to four courses per semester.

**Advising** The committee recognized that the more flexible curricula it proposed would create additional needs for effective student counseling. Its discussion pointed out all the usual difficulties of creating an effective advising system, especially one that works well before the student selects a major. Its only recommendations, however, were that a student be required to have an adviser's approval for a program and that in cases of dispute between student and adviser, the chairman of the Subcommittee on Curriculum be called on to decide the issue.

**Other Matters** The committee proposed that "physical activity" be required for one year, but without grades. This was a compromise between those who proposed retaining the existing two-year requirement and those who argued for complete abandonment of physical education requirements. Finally it was recommended that only four courses taken in an ROTC program be permitted to count for graduation.[4]

**OVERALL IMPACT OF THE PROPOSALS** The specific requirement that the student have a "variety of learning experiences" is unique. The several different formats for instruction have been proposed or are in use elsewhere, but as far as I am aware, Duke is alone in the attempt to formalize them into a structure for undergraduate education. The changes in the distribution requirements are more radical in terms of Duke's past practices than they are in terms of any national norms. Overall, they make possible a rather marked departure from the more traditional structure of "liberal" and "general" education at Duke

---

[4] The Duke report was the only one included in this study which made specific mention of ROTC, and its basic endorsement of the program was hardly challenged in subsequent discussions. This is a striking illustration of the rapidity and the unexpectedness with which an issue can emerge and become a *cause célèbre* in the currently unsettled state of academia.

and may permit—if the student wishes it—rather complete specialization during the undergraduate years.

CONSIDERA-
TION OF
THE REPORT

The committee submitted its report to the Undergraduate Faculty Council on March 22, 1968. Each member of the faculty of arts and sciences received a copy, and copies were given to key student leaders. In addition, the entire text of the report was printed in the student newspaper.

The strategy for considering the report in the Undergraduate Faculty Council was developed by the committee. In general, the approach used was to turn the council into a Committee of the Whole and to proceed on the basis of straw votes. The dean of arts and sciences chaired the meetings, but members of the committee were always present at the front of the room. Even members of the faculty who were quite bitterly opposed to some of the changes which resulted from the committee's report agreed that the discussions "were all done most properly" and were "completely fair." All points of view were given a full hearing, and the committee answered all questions about its reasoning to everyone's satisfaction. The council began by meeting once a week, and by the end of May, when the final votes were taken, it was meeting three times a week. I found no objection to this fairly intensive pace. Although students were involved in the work of the study, they were not involved during consideration by the council. One committee member indicated that student support was not encouraged during this phase because of the fear that faculty votes might be lost. Indeed, it was suggested that one reason for rejection of the committee's proposal to eliminate entirely the foreign language requirement was an editorial urging elimination which appeared in the *Chronicle* (the student newspaper) on the day the vote was taken.

Most of the proposals of the committee were accepted by the Undergraduate Faculty Council. The principal departures were that the council voted to retain a somewhat modified language requirement which the committee had proposed to abolish entirely. Also, the council voted to retain a two-year physical education requirement which the committee had proposed to reduce to one year. Beyond these, only minor modifications were made in the committee's proposals.

OVERALL
RESULTS

The Duke study accomplished most of its objectives and could lead to some significant changes in the processes of education at Duke.

Student enthusiasm was such that some of the changes began to be instituted in the spring semester of 1969 even though they had been accepted by the council for implementation the following fall. The changes appeared to have quite widespread support among the faculty, although some faculty members were not in favor of much of what had been done, feeling that the changes had gone too far. One view expressed was that a truly liberal education had given way to specialization. Another reservation expressed even by some who favored the changes concerned the greater demands implicitly placed on faculty members' time for more careful advising of students and for more time spent in tutorials and small group instruction. Several with whom I talked wondered whether young, untenured faculty members, who are under considerable pressure to publish, would be willing to take the risks required if the full potential of the new curriculum were to be realized. While my search was not extensive, I found no faculty member at Duke who felt that the new proposals had not gone far enough. The opposition was apparently confined entirely to those who felt the proposals moved too far from the *status quo.*

COMMENTARY    Taken in its own terms, the Duke study was most successful. It was done at the right moment to achieve maximum support, for clearly the time had come for liberalization of the curriculum at Duke. Furthermore, given that almost all the opposition came from the "right," it seems that the committee proposed just about enough liberalization.

Given that the changes eliminated—potentially, at any rate—large enrollments in courses which had been previously required, some strong support for the *status quo* was not surprising. On the other hand, the changes have the effect of eliminating much of the need for faculty—as opposed to departmental and individual—decisions about the curriculum. Since it is generally the current fashion for departments rather than faculties to exercise basic control over curriculum, it is not surprising that support was widespread. At Duke, as elsewhere, decisions which permit students more nearly to do their own thing academically also remove some constraints which keep the faculty member from doing his own thing.

The study was carried out with skill. The grant from the Methodist Church gave a certain prestige and importance to the work. The debates in the Undergraduate Faculty Council were conducted with foresight and tact. The committee was always in charge of events, but did not dominate. One faculty member who opposed much of the report spoke glowingly of the conduct of the committee. "There is," he suggested, "no thinking in terms of victory or defeat now that the decisions are made. Everyone is ready to try to make the curriculum work."

# 9. Brown University

## Interim Report—Committee on Educational Principles

Brown University is the smallest member of the Ivy League. It has the academically select student body which characterizes all the Ivy League schools, and in recent years the overwhelming majority of its students have gone on to some sort of postgraduate work. Brown had the foresight, around the turn of the century, to establish a coordinate women's college, Pembroke, and thus has been spared the trauma of "going co-ed," which has lately plagued several members of the Ivy League.

Brown never developed the congeries of graduate and professional schools characteristic of most universities, although a graduate school of arts and sciences has long existed. (Instruction in medicine was recently started, but not within a separate medical school.) Similarly, there are no professional schools at the undergraduate level, although undergraduate instruction in engineering is offered. Except for engineering, the undergraduate curriculum is confined to the liberal arts and sciences, although courses are offered in a number of relatively nontraditional fields such as linguistics and Egyptology. In short, Brown is something more than a traditional liberal arts college, but something less than a typical university center.

Student enrollment at Brown amounts to about 5,000, with about 2,600 men in the college, 1,000 women in Pembroke, and 1,300 men and women in the graduate school. The faculty, numbering about 500, has, on the average, one of the nation's highest salary levels.

Faculty participation in governance at Brown is carried on through the faculty meeting and a structure of standing committees. However, from the mid-1930s until very recently Brown had a tradition of strong presidents, and university policy making was dominated by the president. As in virtually all institutions, the academic departments have an important influence in determinin educational policy. Beginning in 1967, Brown began includin students on certain standing committees.

Until the events described in this case occurred, the bas curriculum and educational policy at Brown were derived large from studies made and actions taken between 1944 and 194 There had, of course, been many modifications during the inte vening years, but the basic elements of the curriculum—a distr bution requirement for general education, a foreign language r quirement, a requirement for proficiency in English compositio and a concentration—had remained essentially in force since 194 (A Brown student could, with approval, design his own concentr tion outside the regular departmental offerings. Few did.) Brow adopted the four-course semester as the normal student load the mid-1930s. Beginning in 1958, Brown began to develop ar offer "university courses," which were intended to provide st dents with an opportunity to integrate knowledge, methods, ar insights from a number of traditional fields.

**THE MAGAZINER REPORT** In the fall of 1966, a Brown sophomore, Ira Magaziner, brougl together a group of students to discuss problems in higher educ tion with the idea of establishing an experimental college a Brown. The group was joined by more students and a number ● faculty members in the second semester of 1966–67 and was mac into a Group Independent Studies Project, which carried academ credit for the participants. The group read widely in the literatu of higher education and made a detailed survey of all the change made (and changes proposed but not made) in educational polic at Brown since 1944. By the end of the academic year 1966–67, tl idea of an experimental college had been more or less abandone and in its place the group was developing proposals for specif changes in undergraduate instruction in Brown as a whole. Durir the summer of 1967, Magaziner and a student colleague, Elli Maxwell, were given a financial grant by the dean of the college t support continuation of their work. Magaziner presented a dra of a rather massive report on the deliberations of the Grou Independent Studies Project to the August, 1967 convention of th National Student Association. During the fall of 1967, Magazine with the help of a number of students, refined his report, which wa entitled *Draft of a Working Paper for Education at Brown.* Tl report, including its extensive bibliography, ran to 413 typewritten pages.

**SPECIFIC PROPOSALS** The Magaziner report[1] was intended to be a basis for a broad discussion of education at Brown rather than a precise blueprint for legislative or administrative action. Consequently, many of its recommendations are merged with broad, philosophical discussions and are neither readily nor fairly summarized. Some of the more central proposals are briefly described in the following pages and should be considered in light of the basic principles which the report develops:

The focusing of education on the individual human being; the encouragement of and the removal or minimizing of pressures which would defeat the seeking of self-knowledge; the developing of intellect and the removal of the narrow professional orientation.

**Curriculum** The curriculum recommendations tended to move simultaneously in the direction of much greater freedom of choice and action for the student and in the direction of greater prescription. The principal case of the latter is in the proposal for required freshman courses. These would "be concerned primarily with an understanding of the values infusing inquiry, and of the centralities of method and conceptual frameworks in approaches to knowledge and phenomena." Such courses would be especially developed in the humanities, social studies, science, and mathematics or formal logic. It was proposed that 20 two-year courses be offered in each of these areas except mathematics and that most freshmen be required to choose one course in each area. In mathematics, a smaller number of one-semester courses would be developed from which each student would make an election. All these freshman courses would have an enrollment of not more than 20, and it was contemplated that most would be taught by two faculty members.

[1] Some of this section will partly duplicate a later summary of proposals formally introduced into the Brown faculty by a subsequent committee. That later summary is necessary to provide a context for the description of the faculty action, but in spite of possible overlap, the following is included to give an indication of the scope and penetration of this rather remarkable document. Student-prepared, it demonstrates a knowledge of educational philosophies and processes at least as substantial as that behind the similar documents prepared by faculty committees elsewhere.

Some freshmen might be excused from one or more of these re
quirements, but it was expected that almost all would take th
courses because they would be "instrumental in orienting th
students away from their high school education."

The study group also proposed abolition of the English com
position requirement and the establishment of intensive 10-wee
institutes for language study in lieu of the traditional cours
approach to the language requirement. Also recommended wer
"third-tier" courses, "designed to combat narrow professionalism
to encourage independence in learning and teaching, to utilize di
ferent ways of approaching knowledge, to integrate variou
approaches to knowledge, to facilitate the relating of ideas t
human concerns and to broaden the student's perspectives."[2] F
nally, there would be provision for both individual independen
study and group independent study.

The study group recommended that the idea of a concentratio
be retained as a basic requirement, but proposed that each studer
be freely permitted to design his own concentration. The area o
concentration, the amount of time devoted to it, and its occurren
in the student's academic career would all be left to the studen
with appropriate counsel.

**Examinations**  The study group proposed that all final examinations be given a
take-home examinations and handed out to students at least on
month before the date due. This was followed with a recom
mendation that final examinations be returned to the students an
that provision be made for a class meeting or individual meetin
between students and professor so that the examination could b
discussed.

**Grading and Evaluation**  The discussion of grading and evaluation covers 61 pages of th
Magaziner report and is a most comprehensive review of th
literature on this subject. A variety of alternative systems an
philosophies are evaluated, and the study group concluded tha
what they called a "dossier system" should be instituted. In th
system grades would not be given, but the faculty would evaluat
all the student's work during a course and give the student a

[2] This was not an entirely new concept. Brown's university courses were a typ
of third-tier course.

detailed a discussion as desirable and possible. At the end of the course the student would select one piece of his work, along with the professor's comments on that work, to become a permanent part of his dossier. The dossier would eventually consist of similar entries for each course taken. However, to provide students with a transition from a grade-oriented high school education, the study group proposed that in the freshman year there be pass-fail grades which would be cooperatively set by faculty members and students.

The study group recognized the extreme difficulty that a single institution would encounter in departing from the nationwide grading system and so proposed, as an interim step, the adoption of a cooperative approach to the regular grading system, according to which the student and the faculty member would meet together and jointly decide on the student's grade for the course. At the same time, the study group announced its intention "to marshal as many forces as possible to convince graduate and professional schools to accept the dossier."

**Teaching** The study group made a rather detailed analysis of teaching and teaching methods and concluded that the widespread use of the lecture should be replaced in many instances by the discussion class and the tutorial. Where lectures were continued it was urged that lecture notes be duplicated and distributed to students so that the lecture could "concentrate on presenting central methods and conceptual frameworks, on providing various interpretations and integration of the material and on communicating an enthusiasm for the area of study."

The study group proposed a formal course evaluation in the form of a "portfolio" for each course. This would include the instructor's written statement about course content, teaching methods, and expectations from students. Each student in the course would be asked to write an evaluation after one month in the course and again at the end of the semester. The first of these would be impressionistic; the second would include factual data about the student and about the conduct of the course. The portfolios on each course would be available to anyone for inspection, but in addition there would be a booklet including "distillations" of the portfolio for each course. The distillation would be made by someone who had neither taken the course nor studied with the professor involved.

**Other Matters**

The report included a discussion of academic counseling, and its principal recommendation was for the exclusive use of upper-class students in counseling freshmen. Both individual and group counseling were recommended. The report also proposed some tentative arrangements for an organized structure for a continuing self-study by the university. The report concluded with a remarkably responsible assessment of the financial implications of its proposals.

**THE STULTZ COMMITTEE**

By the spring of 1967, it had become apparent to the Brown community that these students were serious about educational reform, and as a result the president and the Curriculum Committee of the faculty created a subcommittee to consider curriculum questions generally and the proposals contained in the Magaziner report especially. This subcommittee was charged by the president with "considering innovation and reform in the undergraduate curriculum of the sort that cannot be clearly and specifically related to a single department or small group of departments." While not specifically stated, it was clear to all that the committee had been brought into being essentially to do something about the Magaziner report.

The committee originally consisted of seven faculty members. In November, 1967, President Ray L. Heffner added two students —one of whom was Mr. Magaziner— to the committee. During the year-long life of the committee, three faculty members (including the original chairman) and Magaziner resigned from the committee and were replaced. Professor Stultz, the ultimate chairman, was an original appointee. (The committee eventually became known as the Stultz Committee.) None of these departures was apparently the result of specific disagreements within the committee, although it is true, as the report states, that ". . . difference among members in matters of philosophical viewpoint proved a limiting factor. . . ."

The Stultz Committee tried to come to grips with the desire expressed in the Magaziner report for fully articulated statements of policy on the role of the university and on the nature of under-graduate education, but was unable to do so. Ultimately the group turned its attention to specific issues and indicated that the "recommendations made . . . represent areas of agreement made possible because of congruency of interests and/or beliefs among Subcommittee members of sometimes differing philosophical persuasions. They do not necessarily represent agreements on the principles which underlie them." In spite of its inability to develop any basic philosophy, the committee did state that continuing discussions of curriculum should be based upon a "consideration of these abstract but critical philosophical issues."

The Stultz Committee report was submitted to the president and the Curriculum Committee on May 28, 1968. It made relatively few specific recommendations other than suggesting areas for further study. It did propose that half of the freshman's work be in courses not designed as a basis for further specialized work — courses which would have small enrollments and be concerned primarily with "methods of analysis and modes of thought."

The committee proposed that student-designed concentrations be more readily available and be free of restrictions in terms of number and departmental location of courses taken. Also proposed was a significant increase in the number of university and third-tier courses offered. The committee recommended adoption of an honors-pass-fail grading system and a liberalization of rules concerning final examinations. It was the committee's view that the individual instructor should be entirely free to give or not give final examinations and to decide on the time and form of final examinations given.

The committee's report included very little analysis of the issues involved, and most of its recommendations were stated in a very tentative fashion. There is no indication in the brief (16 pages) report that this particular committee had been able to meet head on and resolve any of the fundamental issues about education which had been raised by the students. The report conveyed no sense of urgency, nor did it give much guidance on specific issues to the Curriculum Committee or to the faculty.

**THE POST-STULTZ INTERLUDE** In the fall of 1968, the students who had initiated the whole process of educational reform came to the conclusion that the Curriculum Committee was unlikely to take any serious action on the proposals of the Stultz Committee. As one said, "We had gotten better response from the trustees (on matters such as university investments) than we were getting from the faculty." Consequently, the group led by Magaziner began to initiate processes for bringing pressure on the faculty to give serious consideration to the proposals for change. Essentially, the students wanted a new committee to be formed and given specific instructions to take action on the Magaziner and Stultz proposals.

A central student committee began to organize a campaign to achieve this end. As a first step they set out to ensure that all faculty members and all students were familiar with the proposals. (A questionnaire sent to the faculty the previous June had brought forth only three replies.) The strategy developed was to have teams of three students call on each member of the faculty for the purpose of ascertaining the faculty member's views on educational change and, if necessary, to explain to him the Magaziner proposals.

Some 200 student volunteers were screened by the central committee. Those selected were given a crash course in the content and philosophy of the Magaziner proposals. They were also put through a trial interview, with a member of the central committee acting as a hostile faculty member. The student teams were assigned to see specific faculty members. In some cases, faculty members—those who taught only graduate students, for example— would not accept an appointment with the students. In such cases, the students persisted, even to the point of appearing during the faculty member's open office hours. After the faculty member had been interviewed, the student team prepared a one-page report on the nature of the interview and the faculty member's general views about changes in Brown's educational policies. These interview records were collected in a central file.

At the same time, the central committee worked for student understanding and support. Meetings were organized in the residence halls, during which a member of the central committee explained and answered questions about the proposals for change. About 50 percent of the student body participated in these meetings, so the central committee organized a door-to-door campaign in which student volunteers called on every member of the student body. As a result of these activities, virtually all students and faculty members were made aware of the nature of the Magaziner proposals.

In spite of the attention directed toward the whole matter by these activities, the Curriculum Committee had not referred any of the Stultz proposals to the faculty. Consequently, the central students' committee organized a series of rallies to push for action. Four of these rallies were held in each of four successive weeks during the fall, with as many as 1,800 students present at a single one. The students made it quite clear that they did not wish to polarize against the faculty or to engage in confrontations, but it was obvious that confrontation was possible if some action were not taken.

As a result of the pressures generated by the students and coming from members of the faculty and administration who wished to move ahead with some changes, President Heffner, in early December, asked Associate Provost Maeder to chair a committee to examine the educational philosophy underlying the undergraduate curriculum at Brown University and to make recommendations concerning this philosophy through the Committee on Curriculum to the faculty as a whole and to the Board of Fellows. The president suggested that enough discussion had already taken place to indicate that a thorough reexamination and redefinition was needed, and he asked for a statement of philosophy and for specific proposals for implementing the philosophy to be prepared in time to permit action by the faculty before the end of the academic year.

The Maeder Committee was chosen by the president in consultation with various members of the faculty, administration, and student body in a departure from Brown's usual practice of having faculty-elected committees. All its members were advocates of educational change—though not necessarily of the specific Magaziner-Stultz proposals. That the chairman was associate provost was an obvious indication by the administration of a commitment to change. While it was not particularly obvious at the time of the appointment of the Maeder Committee, it became clear that there was considerable ill feeling and suspicion among the faculty about the method of appointment and the membership. Because several of its members were administrators or student radicals, many faculty members saw the "student-administration alliance striking again."

**THE MAEDER COMMITTEE** The Maeder Committee began its regular meetings on January 9, 1969, and continued to meet weekly through March. All its meetings were open to all members of the university, and the number of visitors (mostly students) ranged from 4 to 30. The committee met continuously during the first week of April to prepare its report, which was submitted to the faculty on April 10.

The committee sent letters to all faculty members requesting their views on curricular matters, and 37 replies were received. The committee also sent minutes of its meetings to all departments who requested them (23 out of 28 departments did so). After the committee had developed some reasonably firm ideas, it sought to initiate meetings with individual departments to get their ideas and reactions. Eighteen such meetings with two or three committee members and members of a department were held. For some of its work, the committee worked through subcommittees dealing with specific items, and other members of the faculty and student body were added to these subcommittees. Early in March, the committee distributed to faculty and students for discussion drafts of statements on the purposes of the university and on the purposes of undergraduate education. In short, all aspects of the committee work were open and subject to the views and influence of all members of the university.

SPECIFIC
PROPOSALS

The Maeder Committee identified its report as interim because it simply did not have time to cover all relevant items and meet President Heffner's deadline. The interim report included the two statements of principle and recommendations for "modes-of thought" courses, for new concentration requirements, and for a new system of student evaluation. Other items—language requirements, for example—were to be left to a later report.

Modes of
Thought

A principal recommendation of the Maeder Committee was that freshmen devote a considerable portion of their time to modes of-thought courses which would be developed and introduced. In general agreement with the Magaziner report, the committee argued that the freshman year had three major purposes:

(1) to open up pathways of communication between students and faculty which will serve as the basis of meaningful and creative exchange throughout the entire undergraduate experience; . . . (2) to introduce the student to the various methods and concepts which will be useful to him in approaching knowledge and in relating it to personal experience; and . . . (3) to provide a stimulating but relaxed atmosphere in which the student has ample opportunity to explore general areas of knowledge that might interest him.

Conceived of as a way of meeting these requirements, the modes of-thought courses would focus on methods, concepts, and value systems. They would generally transcend the bounds of a particular departmental discipline. Subject matter would change from year to year, and special emphasis would be put on the problem approach. It was proposed that enrollment in a particular course be limited to 20 students and that most teaching be done in discussion groups. Grading would be on only a pass-fail basis. Students would be required to take at least five and not more than seven modes-of thought courses and would have to take at least one in each of four broad areas defined as the humanities, social studies, the natural sciences, and formal thought. A committee for modes-of-thought courses to approve individual course proposals and generally to oversee the program would be appointed.

**Concentration** The Maeder Committee recommended that each student, in consultation with an appropriate faculty member, design a concentration program centered on a discipline, problem, or theme or on some "broad question." The student would be required to prepare a written proposal stating his objectives and listing the courses he intended to take to meet those objectives. Departments and interdepartmental groups of faculty members could establish standard concentration programs which students would elect without individual approval. In essence, the objective of the proposals, in line with the conclusions of the Magaziner report, was to shift emphasis in the concentration from the preprofessional to the liberal. The committee argued that a "liberal, as opposed to specifically pre-professional, concentration is designed to carry out the processes of intellectual and personal development which are at the center of the undergraduate educational experience. In doing this it serves to develop true professionals." No specific maximums or minimums were prescribed for courses making up a concentration.

**University Courses** The Maeder Committee proposed expansion of the university course program "to provide opportunities at a relatively advanced level of analytical competence for the student to achieve a wider perspective than may ordinarily be available in departmental offerings." No specific number of university courses was to be required.

**Independent Study** Removal of the existing limitation on the number of independent study courses that a student might take was recommended. Group independent study was also recommended as a regular part of the curriculum.

**Evaluation of Students** The committee proposed substantial changes in the grading system. All courses except modes-of-thought courses would be graded on a satisfactory–no credit basis or on a letter-grade basis at the option of the instructor. However, in those courses designated as letter-grade courses, the student could choose to have only a satisfactory–no credit grade. In any case, the only letter grades used would be 'A,' 'B,' and 'C', and courses not satisfactorily completed woul‹ not appear on the student's record. Modes-of-thought courses woul‹ be graded, as noted earlier, on only a satisfactory–no credit basi‹ A student would be permitted to withdraw from a course at an‹ time (upon notifying the instructor), and courses withdrawn fron would not be entered on the student's record. To remain in goo‹ standing in the university, the student would have to have satisfac torily completed at least 6 courses by the end of his first year, 1 by the end of his second year, 20 after his third year, and 28 fo‹ graduation. (This represented a reduction from the 32 course‹ traditionally required for graduation at Brown.) The student woul‹ also be evaluated on his performance in his concentration progran

**Summary of Proposals** The Maeder Committee recommendations follow quite closely th more general proposals of the Magaziner report except in the are‹ of student evaluation. (Almost everyone, including Magaziner an‹ his student associates, had become convinced that the proposal for dossiers and cooperative grading were not really workable. These proposals had been under discussion for a couple of year‹ but, at the moment of decision, did represent a very sharp departur‹ from then-current practice. If fully implemented, in letter and i‹ spirit, they would surely represent serious inroads into the com petitive, departmentally oriented approach to undergraduate edu cation at Brown and elsewhere.

**FACULTY ACTION** The introduction of the Maeder report to the Brown faculty brough‹ on what is purported to be the largest and longest faculty meet ing in the history of the university. The meeting went on fo‹ 2½ days and for most of the time was attended by about 350 c‹ the 500 members of the faculty.[3]

Dean Ecklemann, of the college, acted as floor manager for th‹ Maeder proposals, which were initially considered by the facult‹ meeting as a committee of the whole. (This meant, under Brown'‹ rules, that students could observe the meeting.) At the beginnin‹ of the meeting, the statement of principle on the purposes of unde‹ graduate education was moved to the end of the agenda, and th‹ proposals for modes-of-thought courses came before the meetin‹ first. This, as one participant indicated, "gave an opportunity fo‹

[3] To my knowledge, a 70 percent turnout for a faculty meeting discussing edu cational matters is virtually unheard of. Even occupied buildings and polic‹ busts seem not to bring about much greater attendance.

presenting all kinds of substitute proposals which would have gutted the whole thing."

As the discussion got under way, there came to the fore much of the latent faculty opposition to, and bitterness about, the formation and composition of the committee. These were combined with genuine opposition to the changes proposed, with opposition to any change, and with opposition to the changes proposed by students. Much of the specific opposition focused on the distribution requirement which was a part of the modes-of-thought proposal. It was argued that to require certain modes-of-thought courses would be incompatible with the overall goal of freedom and flexibility for the student, which was one of the principal bases for all the proposals. A less well-articulated but apparently much-present fear was that acceptance of the proposal would result in a significant increase in faculty teaching loads. It was also suggested to me that much opposition was essentially a defense of departmental power, for by being explicitly nondepartmental, the courses were a threat to that power.

This first faculty meeting was universally described to me as "bitter and contentious," and in this atmosphere, it was generally agreed, the proposals would have been voted down. However, no votes were taken before adjournment, and at that point the meeting asked President Heffner to cancel all classes the following day and to reconvene the meeting at 9 A.M. As one participant said, "This was the first sign that the faculty was really concerned, for it is not usual to give up 1½ days or more to such discussions."

During the evening and well into the next morning faculty and student supporters of the Maeder proposals met with opponents who they thought would be amenable to a compromise. As a result of much hectic activity during the night, a compromise was worked out which involved acceptance of the modes-of-thought courses without the distribution requirement.

The compromise was introduced at the beginning of the second day of the faculty meeting, and the tone of the meeting changed entirely. As one faculty member put it, "Some of the old divisions seemed to begin to disappear. We may have a new faculty, because for the first time in a long while we began to debate and talk and listen." The compromise on the modes-of-thought courses was accepted, and over the next two days the rest of the Maeder proposals were accepted with only minor modifications. The new curricula and evaluation system were to go into effect in September,

1969. By late May, 1969, some 60 proposals for modes-of-thought courses had been submitted by various faculty members. The Maeder Committee was continuing the development of other recommendations about English composition, foreign languages, and the like.

COMMENTARY  The changes made at Brown represent a potentially significant redirection of undergraduate education at a relatively influential institution. Freedom for, and responsibility of, the individual student in matters relating to his own education will be much increased. An important counterbalance to the specialized, departmental direction of undergraduate education will be brought into being. Whatever one thinks of either of these as objectives, they are markedly different from what most undergraduate education in America has been.

On the other hand, more will have to happen to make the redirection actually, rather than potentially, significant. Students must be willing to accept the freedom and take the responsibility for their education, and the faculty must be willing to guide them —an activity which frequently runs precisely counter to "covering the material." Given what appears to be the conditioning of most students in the secondary school system, it seems that the responsible acceptance of freedom by students would create a need for rather more academic counseling or advising than has been provided thus far by Brown. Without the crutch of a prescribed curriculum, a great many students will require advice from someone. On the other side, if the modes-of-thought courses and the university courses are to have a truly cross-departmental nature, faculty members must devote time and effort to working outside their own areas of specialization. Given the usual reward system of academia, one wonders how much effort in this direction will be made.

It is important to recognize, as well, that these changes were accepted in place of a curriculum that already included most of the more "contemporary" curriculum ideas. There were many opportunities for independent study, a restricted pass-fail option existed, and the university courses provided some offset to departmental specialization. Nor could students complain much about "impersonality" or a "factory atmosphere," as they so often do at the much larger universities.

Whatever may be the ultimate result of the changes in educational policy at Brown, the fact that they were made is surely a tribute to the remarkable tenacity of a group of students and especially to the education and organizing skill of Ira Magaziner.[4] I know of no other instance where major educational change has been entirely initiated and largely pushed through by students. All faculty members with whom I talked agreed that such sweeping changes would not have taken place at this time without the work of the students and especially of Magaziner, which is not to say that all were happy with either the results or the origin of the pressure.

Much of the process by which educational change occurred at Brown was largely uncontrolled by those who normally control such things. It was not a hasty process, certainly. The substance of the Magaziner proposals was known—or available to be known —for many months before the final faculty meetings. The Stultz Committee represented the first attempt of the "official" institution to take charge of the process. Its report was a rather clear indication that there was relatively little basis for agreement within the faculty and relatively little disposition to try to hammer out an agreement on basic principles and specific actions. Unintentionally, no doubt, this report demonstrated that little basic change would be made without pressure—from strong leadership, from massive inspiration, or from threats. In this sense it may be that the Stultz Committee was a necessary step in the process of bringing the institution around to the point of accepting change. Certainly when the Maeder Committee was formed it was clear that the administration had concluded that some changes were inevitable, and Professor Maeder provided important leadership during the latter stages of the process. It also seems likely that the fortuitous adjournment without action after the first faculty meeting provided an opportunity for working out a crucial compromise.

At bottom, however, the changes at Brown are the result of "student power," skillfully and responsibly applied to matters of direct concern to students as students.

---

[4] Brown may perhaps count herself fortunate that this young man has a deep commitment to nonviolence. The fact that the student frustrations over the slow pace of the process did not lead to confrontation of some sort during a period when confrontations were *de rigueur* is remarkable.

# 10. Stanford University
## Study of Education at Stanford

Stanford University has long been the most prominent private university in the Western United States, although until World War II, its prominence had as much to do with athletic and social matters as with academic pursuits. In the past 25 years or so, however, Stanford's prominence has come to be firmly based on its academic excellence—especially in the sciences. In 1967, Stanford enrolled some 11,000 students, of whom about half were undergraduates. While Stanford's graduate students came from all over the world, its undergraduates, who typically had very high academic qualifications, tended to be drawn primarily from upper-middle-class families in the Far West. Although a substantial number of students live off campus, Stanford is basically a residential rather than a commuter university. The university also operates five overseas campuses to which Stanford students may go for six-month periods.

The Stanford faculty has about 1,000 members and includes many persons of national prominence. The faculty offers instruction through seven schools: business, earth sciences, education, engineering, the humanities and sciences, law, and medicine. Undergraduate students are enrolled only in the schools of earth sciences, engineering, and the humanities and sciences, with nearly 90 percent of them in the latter.

During the winter of 1967–68, after a long period of planning, President J. E. Wallace Sterling appointed a steering committee to conduct a study of education at Stanford. The study was carried on through the summer of 1969. No single report was issued, but a succession of volumes dealing with specific topics was issued by the committee beginning in November, 1968. Many of the recommendations included in these volumes were acted upon—wholly or in part—as they came out. The last two volumes were to be issued in the late fall of 1969, after this report was written, and thus the case description given here is necessarily terminated at a point short of the formal conclusion of the study.

Beyond the foregoing, the reader should also bear in mind that the Stanford study was affected more than the other studies by essentially external events. During the past two or three years, the Stanford campus has experienced a succession of upheavals brought on by an increasingly active student body. Protests— sometimes marked by violence—over the war in Vietnam, recruiting on campus, and the activities of various institutes and the university have followed one another during the course of the study. A sit-in by students in the spring of 1968 brought on a divisive controversy over the granting of amnesty to the students, a controversy in which the chairman of the study committee played a prominent role. Other sit-ins during the winter and spring of 1969, which were ended by police action and the suspension of a number of students, seriously diverted attention from consideration of proposals made by the study. During the period of the study, the Stanford community was becoming more and more radicalized, and it is not easy to isolate the effects of this on the progress of, and response to, the study.

Another unfortunate and possibly consequential occurrence was that the chairman of the steering committee, Prof. Herbert L. Packer, suffered a serious stroke just at the moment when some of the most important of the committee's proposals were being introduced and considered by the university as a whole. In short, the isolation of cause and effect is more uncertain in the case of the Stanford study than has been true of any of the others reviewed here.

**ORIGIN OF THE STUDY** The decision to undertake a wide-ranging study of education at Stanford was made largely by President Sterling in response to a number of different factors. One of these was the evidence of growing student unrest. During 1965 and 1966, when the idea for the study was developing, Stanford had not had disturbances of the magnitude of the Free Speech Movement at neighboring Berkeley, but there had been a number of protests over one thing or another. President Sterling felt that these indicated a need for a review of the university's educational processes.

A second factor in President Sterling's decision was his concern over an imbalance in Stanford's educational programs which had been developing since the early 1950s. Under the leadership of then-Provost Frederick E. Terman, Stanford had rapidly developed its faculty and facilities in the sciences and the "hard" social sciences—largely through successful tapping of government support for research in these areas. As has been true of so many universities, there had not been a parallel development in the humanities and the "soft" social sciences. The largest number of undergraduates was enrolled in these latter areas, while most of the activity in the sciences was at the graduate level. Thus the president concluded that there was a need to restore some balance between these areas and to give more attention to undergraduate education generally.

Beyond these considerations was the fact that there had been no comprehensive review of undergraduate curricula for some 10 years except for the introduction of a modest program of freshman seminars. There was a widespread feeling among faculty members —and especially among the younger ones—that the regular academic committees were not encouraging any real change and that it was very difficult for anyone else to bring about even modest change. Students had also begun to raise the issue of the need for change. Thus, while President Sterling's decision to embark on a study of education at Stanford was not made in response to any widespread demand, the announcement appears to have been generally well received by the faculty and, initially, by the students.

ESTABLISH-
MENT OF A
SENATE

One event which was independent of, but very closely related to, the study was the establishment of a Faculty Senate at Stanford in 1968. Prior to that time, faculty policy making had been ostensibly in the hands of the Academic Council, which included all faculty members above the rank of instructor. As might be expected with such a large body, most power was actually in the hands of a nine-member executive committee which represented the several schools and certain other constituencies in the university. As a matter of practice, membership of this committee had for a long time been drawn from a relatively small group of senior faculty members. Furthermore, Stanford had had, since its founding, a tradition of strong presidents. As a result of these conditions, faculty involvement in university policy making was limited, and there had not been any great demand to expand it. As one faculty member put it, "Stanford is a very discipline-oriented university, and few faculty members are much interested in general questions of university policy."

Professor Herbert L. Packer was a member of the executive committee in 1966–67 and urged that a larger, more representative body be created. The executive committee proceeded to develop a charter for a senate, and the latter was accepted by the faculty in the spring of 1968. In a rare display of academic statesmanship, the executive council put itself out of business.

The senate consists of 50 members elected by the schools and various constituencies in the university. Members of the central administration and the deans of the schools are *ex officio,* non-voting members. The number of senators from a constituency is determined by the relative number of students and the relative number of faculty members in the constituency. A possibly unique feature of the Stanford senate is that senators are elected from each constituency by a system of proportional representation. This resulted, in the first senate election, in a large number of relatively junior faculty members winning seats. Several faculty members suggested that the senate membership, in 1968–69, was rather "to the left" of the faculty as a whole. The senate can be overruled by the Academic Council, with senate actions being referred to the larger body on petition of one-third of the senate or 50 members of the faculty at large.

The existence of the senate was a crucial element in the conduct of the study at Stanford. It seems clear that the old executive committee was too narrowly based to have permitted much confidence in its decisions about the recommendations of the study. Similarly, the Academic Council was much too large to be an effective legislative body. The creation of a representative body of reasonable size to deal with recommendations emanating from the study was an obviously necessary step at Stanford.

**PRELIMINARY DECISIONS** Certain decisions which were preliminary to the actual conduct of the study, and yet part of its overall process, were made by President Sterling and his associates. Among these decisions were the appointment of a vice-provost for academic planning, the structuring of the form of the study, and selection of the steering committee. Each of these is discussed below.

**Vice-provost for Academic Planning** Early in the planning process, President Sterling created the post of vice-provost for academic planning and chose Professor Packer of the School of Law to fill it. It was the president's intention that Professor Packer would assume the leading role in the conduct of the study of education and that he would be the member of the central administration directly responsible for the consideration and implementation of recommendations ultimately resulting from the study. Thus Professor Packer was involved in most of the early decisions about the way in which the study would be done and who would be involved. Furthermore, with this appointment, an important step was taken before the study began toward ensuring that it would not be simply reported upon and forgotten.

**Structure of the Study** A first decision of the president and Professor Packer was that the success of any study would depend in part upon the involvement of as many members of the Stanford community as possible— faculty and students. This, in turn, led to a decision to have as much of the study as possible done through topic committees. The central committee would function partly as a steering committee. The steering committee would itself consider the academic programs of the university, but other important areas such as admissions, advising, and campus life would be studied by topic committees, with the steering committee maintaining an overview of their work. In some cases, members of the steering committee would also be members of topic committees, and it was understood that the steering group could submit recommendations contrary to those of the topic committees.

It was intended that this process would involve larger numbers of people in the actual conduct of the study and, in addition, would make it possible to avoid what Provost Richard Lyman called the "syndrome of the big fat volume which sits on the shelf." Topic committee reports were put out as the overall study progressed in the hope that action might occur with respect to many issues while the study was going on. It was also intended that the topic committee reports, along with the steering committee's views on the particular issues, would be published in a series of separate volumes.

**Selection of the Steering Committee** Membership of the steering committee was set at six faculty members and three student members. The faculty members were selected by President Sterling and Professor Packer in consultation with others. In general, those chosen were men who were influential in the faculty and who had been personally involved in educational experimentation and innovation. The fact that only one faculty representative from the humanities was included among the committee members and that several of the others represented professional, applied disciplines was a matter of consternation to some, who were concerned about how well these men would represent a faculty whose membership was much more heavily concentrated in the humanities and the sciences. On the other hand, all those outside the committee with whom I talked agreed that there was little dissatisfaction expressed over the actual appointments when they were made. All the members were widely respected, and as one faculty member put it, "They were very surefooted appointments."

*Student appointments*

The committee did, however, encounter some real difficulties over student membership. For at least two or three years prior to the initiation of the study of education, Stanford had been putting students on committees on an informal, advisory basis. The usual procedure for selecting student members was to ask the student government organization for nominations. At the time the steering committee was being formed, however, the student government leaders were very radical students, and President Sterling decided that student members selected in the usual way would not be particularly helpful to the work of the committee. At the same time, the administration wished to avoid the charge of having handpicked some "Uncle Toms" from among the student body. Consequently,

TABLE 7    *Membership of the Steering Committee for the Study of Education at Stanford, Stanford University*

| *Name and rank* | *Field* | *Age group** | *Years on Stanford faculty* | *Degrees from Stanford* |
|---|---|---|---|---|
| Norton T. Batkin, undergraduate | Philosophy | Under 33 | | None |
| James F. Gibbons, professor | Electrical engineering | 34–41 | 11 | Ph.D. |
| Albert H. Hastorf, professor | Psychology | 42–49 | 7 | None |
| Joshua Lederberg, professor | Genetics | 42–49 | 10 | None |
| Marc Mancall, associate professor | History | 34–41 | 3 | None |
| Michael Menke, graduate student | Physics | Under 33 | | None |
| Anne Osborn, graduate student | Medicine | Under 33 | | A.B. |
| Herbert L. Packer, professor | Law | 42–49 | 13 | None |
| Leonard Schiff, professor | Physics | 50–57 | 21 | None |
| Robert Hind, associate dean | Education | 42–49 | 8 | B.S., Ph.D. |

*Ages and years at the institution are given as of the time the committee was first convened.

students were asked to enter a competition for membership on the steering committee. All students were invited to apply in writing, giving a statement of their interests and qualifications. About 80 students did apply, and Professor Packer and Robert Hind, the staff director for the study, screened all these applications and selected a number of likely candidates for interviews. The student government leaders, unhappy at being bypassed, condemned this procedure as paternalistic and began to organize a boycott of the study and all its works. The issue was finally resolved when Professor Packer invited two of the radical student leaders to join in the review of applications and the interviews. This proposal was accepted, but the students did not, in fact, participate in many of the interviews. The furor created by these events never did completely die down, however, and for a time clouded the subsequent work of the committee. This was the first of several occasions in the life of the steering committee when some faculty members felt that the committee was selling out to students or using students to overcome the "stodgy faculty."

**SUMMARY OF THE RECOMMENDATIONS** Because of the way in which the Stanford study was conducted, it is not possible to describe separately the processes of developing and considering proposals. The two were, to a considerable extent, being carried on at the same time. Consequently, the final recommendations coming from the study are summarized here, prior to a description of how the study was carried on.

The Stanford study is more all-embracing in its scope than any of the other studies reviewed here. Some indication of that scope is given by the following list of the 10 volumes of the study. The number of specific recommendations included in the volume is given in parentheses.

I   *The Study and Its Purposes*—38 pages (1)

II   *Undergraduate Education*—109 pages (30)

III   *University Residences and Campus Life*—75 pages (20)

IV   *Undergraduate Admissions and Financial Aid*—81 pages (28)

V   *Advising and Counseling*—104 pages (16)

VI   *The Extra Curriculum*—93 pages (24)[1]

VII   *Graduate Education*—125 pages (13)

[1] Released after this report was written.

**VIII** *Teaching, Research, and the Faculty* — 144 pages (17)[2]

**IX** *Study Abroad* — 79 pages (7)

**X** *Government of the University* — 113 pages (44)

While the publication of separate volumes may have prevented the appearance of the "big fat volume" to which Provost Lyman referred, the over 900 pages of prose and the 200 specific proposals generated by the Stanford study far exceed the production of any of the other studies. The following summary focuses primarily on volumes II, III, IV, V, and X, which deal with those issues which are also the concern of the other studies included in this review.

**Curriculum**    The study recommended that the general education program, which had involved requirements in English, contemporary civilization, foreign language, and mathematics and which had a rather complex distribution requirement, be greatly simplified. In its place, all freshmen would have a one-semester course in historical studies, a one-semester writing experience, and a tutorial in the first semester. (All these could be met in a single course.) The tutorial would be directed toward conveying the style of intellectual inquiry in the teacher's field or toward showing the relationships between fields. In addition, each student would elect two semester-length courses in the humanities, two in the social sciences, and two in the natural sciences. No department could prescribe more than one-half of the student's total program,[3] and students could design their own majors. Carefully controlled field work done off campus would also be permitted for academic credit.

**Curriculum Administration**    The topic committee on university governance and the steering committee recommended the appointment of a dean of undergraduate studies whose functions would be "to exercise continuing review of Stanford's education of undergraduates, to support and maintain what is good, to aid in the renovation of what is inadequate, and to stimulate and assist educational innovation." The dean would have "budgetary leverage" and a voice in decisions

---

[2] Released after this report was written.

[3] The problem of the accredited engineering programs was met by permitting them to exceed this limit but also requiring the engineering school to offer a major program which would meet the 16-course limitation.

about faculty appointment and retention. It was also recommended that he be supported by a standing committee on undergraduate education. This committee would replace two existing committees. The dean would also be responsible for a general education college which the report recommended. This college would not be a replacement for regular programs, but would develop a common, integrated general education program for students who wished to follow this approach rather than that of departmentally based programs.

**Calendar and Grades** The committee proposed that Stanford convert from the quarter system to the semester system, with four courses per semester being the normal student load. The conventional grading system would be abandoned under the committee's recommendations and, in essence, replaced with a "pass-erase" system. That is, failures would not be recorded, and, subject only to the consent of the instructor and the department, any course could be taken on a pass-erase basis. In any case, only A, B, and C would be given as letter grades. Students would be permitted to receive credit for any course by passing a written or oral examination.

**Advising** The Stanford committee recognized that advising is generally inadequate because many faculty members regard it as unimportant or feel quite incompetent once they are called upon to give advice outside their own discipline. Consequently, the committee proposed to give advising a specific and important academic focus by creating an advising office, headed by an associate dean of undergraduate studies, with responsibility for all aspects of undergraduate advising. An Academic Senate standing committee on advising would also be brought into being, and the university catalogue would be revamped to include a description of the advising system in use in each department. Perhaps more important was the recommendation that performance as adviser be officially and formally taken into account in faculty appointment and promotion decisions. Finally, the committee proposed that the instructor in the tutorial which each freshman would take be the student's adviser. After his freshman year, the student would choose a faculty or staff member as his university adviser. (The latter would have to agree to be chosen.) Suggestions for experimentation by departments with student advisers were also made.

**Residences** The study argued that "living and learning, social and intellectual life should not be separate but together" and that students should be free to select the living arrangements most suited to their needs. Several proposals were made to permit greater realization of these goals. Among them were the introduction of coeducational residences and the reduction of occupancy rates in dormitories. The committee also recommended the abandonment of facilities for faculty residences in dormitories and the construction of apartments for junior faculty members and graduate students immediately adjacent to undergraduate dormitories. Since the Stanford campus is rather isolated from the commercial districts of Palo Alto, the university was urged to develop a "main street" on the campus. A standing committee of the senate would be established to oversee residential programs and community facilities.

**Admissions** The topic committee and the steering committee were both much concerned with changing what was widely regarded as the homogeneous nature of the Stanford undergraduate student body. Increased recruiting activity among minority groups and expansion of financial aid were proposed as principal ways of achieving this goal. The committee also proposed a new system for selecting freshmen which was intended to get, as one member of the committee put it, "a well-rounded student body rather than a body of well-rounded students." This would be done by indicating a number of wanted characteristics—high school academic achievement, athletic ability, and musical talent, for example—and selecting a portion of each freshman class from among applicants who were outstanding in one but not others of these characteristics. Part of the class would continue to be admitted as all-round students. Details of these proposals would be left to a senate committee on admissions and financial aid.

**Administration and Governance** In addition to the key proposal for a dean of undergraduate education, the topic committee on government of the university made a number of recommendations which were generally aimed at opening up and strengthening the administrative processes at Stanford. Faculty and students would participate in the selection of deans, department heads, and other academic administrators. The term in office of these administrators would be limited. Similarly, faculty membership on standing committees and service as chairmen of such committees would be for limited periods. Students would be regular members of all standing committees except those concerned with faculty promotion and tenure. A number of recommendations concerning the Board of Trustees would have the effect of broadening the base from which board members are drawn and of making the board more familiar with the nature of the university.

**Summary** The Stanford study involves 10 volumes and over 200 recommendations. As might be expected, the quality of the volumes varies somewhat, with some making much more penetrating analyses and offering much more imaginative proposals than others. Overall, the proposals concerned with undergraduate education would have the effect of giving the student considerably greater freedom. Furthermore, both the character of the undergraduate student body and the way in which students live and work while at Stanford would be changed by the committee's proposals. Since the volume dealing with teaching and the faculty had not been completed at the time of this writing, one cannot evaluate that aspect of the study, but it may be observed that most of the other proposals about curriculum are largely structural. If any of the problems of education at Stanford are related to the behavior of faculty members and their attitudes toward students and toward the substance and processes of teaching and learning, it is not particularly apparent in the proposals made thus far.

The other principal thrust of the recommendations, and not only of those specifically concerned with government, would result in a more open system of policy making than Stanford previously had. It was a clearly stated hope of the committee that a more open system would also be more responsive to the need for ongoing reassessment and change of policy.

**CONDUCT OF THE STUDY** The steering committee began its work in January, 1967, although for a few weeks its efforts were devoted largely to organizational matters. A first step was to prepare a list of some 250 questions to which answers would be sought. These questions were publicized throughout the campus, and responses to them were solicited. At this same early point, several topic committees were set up to consider, among others, such questions as advising, admissions, financial aid, housing, teaching, and university government. Many of these topic committees had subcommittees, and all told, more than 200 faculty members, students, and administrative staff members were involved in their work. The members of these groups were selected mainly by the steering committee and were chosen with an eye both to their interests and qualifications and to their standing and influence in the community.

In March, the steering committee began its own deliberations on the academic programs—graduate and undergraduate. There was some controversy within the committee about whether it should begin with a broad exploration of the nature of the university or with an examination of specific educational programs. The latter approach was ultimately adopted. The committee met weekly for the most part except during the summer of 1967, when it met three times each week. According to its members, it was an effective and generally compatible working group, though it was plagued by absenteeism as members left the campus from time to time for periods of varying length. Partly for this reason, but also because of his involvement in the preliminary planning, and especially because of his widely recognized ability, Professor Packer seems to have dominated the Stanford study rather more than the chairmen of most of the other studies did. Several members commented on the invaluable contribution to the committee's work made by Norton Batkin, an undergraduate student.

In line with the overall intention that the study be conducted with maximum exposure and involvement, the committee made extensive surveys about many issues through questionnaires, staff studies, and interviews. Several open hearings were held on a number of issues, during which the committee heard the views of interested persons and groups. At least some committee members felt that these latter were too unstructured and, except for giving people an opportunity to speak their pieces, contributed little to the process. The interviews, as well, seem to have been not entirely successful. Apparently, the steering committee's view of who should be consulted on any particular issue did not always coincide with others' views—especially the views of those not consulted. There were also some feelings expressed to me that the steering committee consulted others after it had made up its own mind on issues. The chairman of one important committee resigned as a result of such feelings. On the other hand, the openness with which the committee generally worked and the involvement of others in its activities appear to have committed many to its proposals—at least to their intent, if not their detail—before they finally appeared.

The proposal of the steering committee to create the post of dean of undergraduate studies was particularly contentious—especially in the School of Humanities and Sciences—and there was an attempt in that school to block any action by the steering committee. The attempt was narrowly defeated, largely through the efforts of younger faculty members. Members of the foreign language departments were equally aroused by the revelation that the steering committee intended to recommend abolition of the language requirement for undergraduates. Dissatisfaction with the preliminary work of the topic committee concerned with university government resulted in the formation of a parallel committee by the Stanford chapter of the AAUP, which issued its own report in the fall of 1968. Ultimately the work of the two groups was reconciled, and the report of the AAUP committee was included in the final report of the committee.

The work of many of the topic committees was much less contentious. For example, many of the recommendations of the topic committee concerned with residences and campus life were being implemented before the final report actually came out. Principal among these was the creation of coeducational dormitories and the conducting of regular classes in the dormitories.[4]

Admission of minority-group students and acceptance of student-designed interdepartmental majors were two other suggestions arising from the study which were implemented prior to formal recommendation by the committee.

**CONSIDERATION OF VOLUME II** The steering committee's own report on undergraduate education was published in November, 1968. While none of the committee's reports was addressed to any particular group, it was understood that the newly created senate would consider the proposals in this report. The steering committee of the senate asked the study committee to divide its recommendations into blocks of more or less closely related issues. The senate steering committee then appointed four floor-management committees, one for each of the blocks of proposals. These latter groups were to put the proposals

[4] One faculty member pointed out that these ideas had long been accepted and advocated by many in the university, but had always been forestalled by "the bureaucracy's contention that it would take at least two years to change men's johns into women's johns." The topic committee's work appears to have been sufficiently forceful, for the decision was implemented in just a couple of months' time. Apparently, the "john" problem was amenable to solution.

into appropriate form for legislation and to lead the senate discussions on them.

During this same period, the senate moved to ensure student
participation by asking the student government to create a Student
Education Council. Issues introduced into the senate were simultaneously introduced into this 40-member student group. The two
bodies would discuss the issues in joint meetings, but would vote
on them separately. In the case of contrary positions, a joint
"amelioration committee" would be appointed to try to reconcile
differences and develop a mutually acceptable position. If there
was still disagreement after this step, the senate's position would
rule. By the fall of 1969, a number of issues had gone through this
conference process, and while senate votes did not always entirely
reflect the students' position, no serious impasses had occurred.

This process of consideration of the recommendations of the
steering committee about undergraduate education began in the
winter of 1969, but before it really got under way, two rather shat-
tering events took place. One of these was a long series of student
sit-ins and other protests directed against the Stanford Research
Institute and the Applied Electronics Laboratories. These protests
were concerned primarily with the university's involvement in war-
related research—especially secret research. As a result, much of
the university's energies during the winter and spring were devoted to crisis management and to the development of new university policies governing research. The *Study of Education at
Stanford* (SES) report was not forgotten during this period, but
consideration of it generally took a back seat.

The second occurrence was the serious stroke suffered by Professor Packer in March, which left the work of SES leaderless.
Just prior to this, Prof. Robert Hind, who had been deeply involved
in the study as staff director, left Stanford for a new position. In
addition, several of the other steering committee members were
absent from the campus. As a result of these circumstances, any
action was more or less halted for a time. Ultimately, Prof. James
Gibbons, a committee member, took over the administration of
the unfinished work of the committee. (Two of the ten volumes
had not been completed at the time of Professor Packer's illness.)
In May, Professor Gibbons was officially designated acting chairman of the steering committee.

As a result of these occurrences, much of the momentum behind
the study was lost, and by the end of May no action had been taken

by the senate. In an attempt to regain some momentum, Professor Gibbons and the senate steering committee sent to all members of the senate and the Student Education Council a list of all the recommendations introduced and not acted upon. The members of each group were asked to indicate whether they favored, opposed, or would like more discussion on each issue. (The responses generally indicated a much higher degree of uncertainty on the part of faculty members than of students, the latter generally having a positive position on most issues. Whether this indicates that faculty members were more aware of the ramifications or simply less familiar with the recommendations is not clear. Both views were expressed to me by faculty members.)

As a result of this questionnaire, consideration of the proposals was recognized and taken up in earnest, beginning in the summer of 1969. New requirements for graduation were passed. Under these, the only specific requirement which all Stanford undergraduates must meet is to have one year of work in the natural sciences, one in the social sciences, and one in the humanities and, for at least two quarters, a "writing experience" (which need not be in a course offered by the English department). No particular courses are identified as meeting these latter requirements, and any or all of them can be met by examination only. This change involved elimination of the language requirement, which was not accepted without contention. The senate voted narrowly in favor of the abolition of required language study. Members of the language departments then petitioned for a review of the decision by the Academic Council. In the council, the petitioners proposed a faculty-wide referendum, and the proposal was defeated by a narrow margin.[5]

Another issue which had been the focus of much controversy since early in the steering committee's work was resolved when the senate voted to ask the president to appoint a dean of undergraduate studies. The senate action provided that the dean would have a budget and a voice in promotion, tenure, and hiring decisions. The president has appointed a committee to select that dean. This decision was made with very little debate in the senate. Apparently, the long period of discussion while the proposal was being formulated had resolved the issue. This is also an issue which students

[5] In the fall term of 1969, the first without a language requirement, enrollments in introductory language courses increased over previous years.

took to heart, and I was told that they energetically and effectively campaigned for it.

In October, 1969, the proposal to switch from a quarter system to four-course semesters had still not been resolved. (The proposal also involved a change from units to courses as the basis for academic bookkeeping.) Several persons to whom I talked said that the issue had been "debated endlessly." At Stanford, as elsewhere, those in the humanities and social sciences appear to favor the semester system, with mathematicians, scientists, and engineers preferring the quarter system. Students favor the quarter system by a wide margin.

The proposal to change the grading system had still not been acted upon. The recommendation for expansion of the freshman tutorial program had been tabled because of the cost involved. No decision had been taken on the proposal for establishing a "general education college" on the grounds that nothing should be done until the dean for undergraduate studies had been appointed.

Proposals made in other volumes on admissions, advising, and overseas campuses had been dealt with primarily by referring them to the newly created standing committees of the senate. The volumes titled *The Extra Curriculum* and *Teaching, Research, and the Faculty* were to be issued shortly after October, 1969.

**OVERALL RESULTS**

Since many specific issues raised by the *Study of Education at Stanford* have not yet been considered, it is neither possible nor fair to attempt an assessment of results, though some tentative conclusions are possible.

To an outsider, the most significant result is the extent to which Stanford has been opened up. One has the distinct impression that prior to SES, decision making at Stanford was largely in the hands of an oligarchy of senior administrators and senior faculty members. One faculty member said to me that he had to serve on a Stanford committee to learn how the chairmen of congressional committees really wield their power. There is no doubt at all that SES has changed all this—not only at the top, but throughout the university, for the old situation was at least as much a result of faculty indifference about policy making as of the desire of a few to control it. At the same time, it must be recognized that the opening up of Stanford is also attributable to the growing activism of its students. SES did not start this—indeed, it was partly a response to it—but certainly utilized it and gave it issues on which to focus.

In narrowly educational terms, the achievements of the study are not yet terribly dramatic. At Stanford, as elsewhere, general education requirements have been liberalized, but it does not appear that much has yet been done by many departments to develop and introduce new courses and programs which may be more nearly related to the needs of students—especially freshmen—than departmental introductory courses appear to be. Perhaps the new dean of undergraduate studies will bring this about.

How effective the new deanship is remains to be seen. Certainly Stanford has attempted to put more teeth into this position than other institutions have. The fact that the newly appointed dean of the School of Humanities and Sciences, Albert Hastorf, was a member of the steering committee and a supporter of the new post should surely help in working out relationships between the two positions, which, potentially at any rate, are points of conflict.

A most significant achievement appears to have been the change in the philosophy behind university residences and the operational changes intended to implement that philosophy. The growing tendency, in recent years, for students to want to live off campus appears to have been reversed by the changes in the university's approach to on-campus living. It is no discredit to SES to say that its role in this change was more facilitative than innovative.

All in all, the greatest achievement of the Stanford study thus far appears to be the creation of a climate for change. Most people at Stanford also feel that through the introduction of a senate and other related changes in the system of governance, there has also been created a structure for change. The reader of the rest of the cases included in this volume may conclude that this is not necessarily so. The Stanford senate benefits at the moment from newness, but one may suggest that such structures can fairly quickly become barriers to change which are as fully effective as an oligarchy. In terms of specific changes and especially those directly related to educational policy, the record is incomplete.

COMMENTARY   The Stanford study is more comprehensive and complex in design and execution than any of those conducted by the larger institutions. It has gone on for well over three years and will surely continue for some time to come. Everyone with whom I talked agreed that the study's cost in time and energy consumed had been enormous, but all except one person agreed that it had been worth it. Everyone also seemed to feel that the value lay essentially in a change in the atmosphere and structure of the university, rather than in specific educational changes.

In spite of the fact that a tremendous amount of attention has been given to undergraduate education at Stanford,[6] there has been little direct confrontation with the nature of that education in the broadest sense. As in the other cases, specific changes have been approved or rejected without any serious thought having been given to the context in which they were being considered. It seems revealing that a host of issues about education have been considered without the volume on teaching having been issued—nor was there any discussion of that issue, which must surely be at the heart of undergraduate education.

On the other hand, it is quite possible that without the sit-ins, Professor Packer's illness, and the departure of Professor Hind, the consideration of the SES proposals would have followed a different course. The very complexity of the study required a strong guiding hand and a good deal of undivided attention from those who would act upon it. Conditions made both of these requirements nearly impossible to meet, and the fact that the study did not simply die on the vine in the spring of 1969 is clear evidence of the determination of many to see it through.

Student participation was built into the study from the start, and some students apparently did yeoman service. Several persons with whom I talked at Stanford suggested that indirect student influence was perhaps more significant. They suggested that without the threat of student pressure, there would have been less acceptance by the faculty of the need for change. Others to whom I put this observation for their reaction vigorously denied it.

The *Study of Education at Stanford* has certainly achieved its objective of having the university examine itself in a fairly thorough-going fashion. It has helped to bring about a number of important changes and has, at least for the present, created a structure for policy making and administration which is much more likely to ensure continued reassessment than the Stanford structure before the study began.

[6] The volume on graduate study appears to have had little impact, and several observed to me that its quality was not up to that of other volumes.

# 11. *Two Partial Cases*

The following situations are not reported in as much detail as the foregoing. For one reason or another it was not possible to interview all key people or to obtain all the data necessary to support a complete case study. However, because the discussions in the following chapters do draw on these studies as well as those previously presented, they are given here in brief outline.

**COLUMBIA COLLEGE** *The Reforming of General Education,* by Daniel Bell, is unique among the reports included in this study because it was written by an individual rather than by a faculty or student-faculty committee. (I know of only one other recent study done by an individual — that by Professor Sussman at Rutgers.) Bell's report is also unique compared with the others because it is much more philosophical in its tone and approach and includes as well a historical essay on part of the general education movement. Finally, Bell's study is more narrowly focused than any of the others, being concerned only with general education. This focus, however, did not keep Bell from commenting on many of the issues more specifically dealt with in other studies.

Bell's study is the "oldest" of those reviewed here, having been started in 1963, though it was published after the Berkeley report came out. Both the idea for the study and the decision to undertake it came from David Truman, who had recently been appointed dean of Columbia College. The decision was made without consultation, according to Dr. Truman, and was precipitated by the unexpected availability of Professor Bell and financial support from The Carnegie Corporation of New York. According to both Dr. Truman and Professor Bell, there was no particular demand for change at Columbia at the time, nor did any crises provoke the study. Dr. Truman told me that he wanted to "needle the faculty and provoke debate" and that he felt he could accomplish this best with a one-man study. He thought that one man could clarify issues and present a sharp point of view, whereas a committee report would inevitably involve compromises.

**Summary of Proposals**  In many ways, Bell's discussions are much more important than his specific proposals, and the following summary does not do justice to the report as a whole. Basically, Bell reaffirmed the idea of a uniform, required general education program, and his specific proposals were aimed at updating and strengthening that program. Specifically, he proposed extending Columbia's contemporary civilization sequence from a year to 1½ years, the first term to deal with Greek and Roman history, and the second and third with the rest of history in one of three tracks — economic, social, or political. These three semesters would be followed by a semester in one of the social sciences. The two-semester humanities course would also be extended to include a third semester introducing modern and contemporary art.

Bell proposed eliminating the required course in English composition and making competence in composition a prerequisite for admission. He further recommended a required year of science in either mathematics-biology or mathematics-physics. Bell also proposed that "double-track" majors be available for students who do not want to become professionals in a field and that in his senior year, each student take a number of "third-tier courses that would 'brake' the drive toward specialization" (Bell, 1966, p. 293). Through all these changes, Bell also emphasized his concern for a shift in content of courses toward conceptual inquiry, "the formation and operation of rules as they govern the meaning of statements and the behavior of human beings."

**Disposition**  Bell's report was presented as an essay rather than as a typical report to a faculty. He stated to me that he was concerned with stimulating consideration of the theme of what knowledge is essential for a postindustrial society. He was not concerned with educational planning as such and thus did not cast up detailed legislative proposals. In practice, this meant that consideration of the report by the college faculty was somewhat difficult. The chapters of the study dealing specifically with changes at Columbia were circulated to faculty members in mimeographed form and discussed in three informal faculty meetings in the spring of 1966. The meetings were not particularly well attended. Professor Bell was present at these meetings, but deliberately played a very limited role in them. He suggested to me that he wanted to avoid seeming to have adopted fixed positions and that active involvement in the discussions might make him seem too much like a proselytizer and defender of his own views.

Ultimately, the Committee on Instruction, the key committee of the college faculty, took the report under advisement. Ad hoc committees were set up to consider the proposals for third-tier courses and the contemporary civilization sequence. During much of this period Professor Bell was on leave, and in June of 1967 Dr. Truman moved from the deanship to the vice-presidency of the university. The two people who were most identified with the study were not heavily involved in the discussions of it. Furthermore, in spite of Bell's concern with the theme of the study, the specifics were a source of faculty concern. Natural scientists, especially, were not happy with some of the proposals for science courses, according to Dr. Truman.

Some revisions were eventually made in the contemporary civilization sequence, and individuals experimented with third-tier courses. By the spring of 1968, however, when other matters came to occupy Columbia's attention, there had been no further formal consideration of Bell's study by the college faculty. As is true of all the studies, there was some localized response to *The Reforming of General Education,* but on the whole it seems to have had little college-wide impact.

**UNIVERSITY OF CALIFORNIA AT LOS ANGELES** This study was done by a committee of seven faculty members. The formal decision to do it was made by the Academic Senate in May, 1966. That there was no particular urgency behind the decision is suggested by the fact that the committee was not appointed until five months later. Some people at UCLA suggested that the decision was a response to the wide publicity received by Berkeley's Muscatine report, and others indicated that it involved an attempt by some faculty members to review and perhaps overturn certain decisions recently made in connection with the university's shift from the semester to the quarter system.

Some members suggested to me that the committee never became an effective working group. As one of them put it, "We spent most of our time arguing about whether it was our job to make statements about educational philosophy." Individual members offered to resign on more than one occasion. A preliminary report presented orally to a weekend meeting of a number of key faculty members was badly received, and this had at least one effect on the final report. The latter, called *Report of the Committee on Academic Innovation and Development,* is very much shorter and much less unified and includes much less analysis than any of the others reviewed. It sets forth 51 recommendations, and these are presented along with supporting discussion in just 44 typewritten pages — many of which are double-spaced. Few of the recommendations are readily susceptible to legislation or to specific administrative action. Virtually everyone to whom I talked at UCLA described the report as "hortatory."

**Summary of Proposals**

Overall, the report displays a concern for making the orientation of general education courses and curricula less professional and for providing greater freedom of choice for students in designing programs. In addition, several recommendations are directed toward the greater encouragement of experimentation and toward finding ways of making instruction and student life in a large university less impersonal.

The committee asked for the establishment of a Council on Educational Development which would have the authority to grant temporary approval to special and experimental courses and programs initiated by faculty members or students. It also proposed the establishment of a University College which would offer two-year programs in addition to, and different from, the regular freshman-sophomore programs. Introductory courses for nonspecialists in addition to regular introductory courses were proposed, and it was recommended that the breadth or distribution requirements, instead of being tied to the traditional divisions of the curriculum, be met simply by any 10 courses "sufficiently independent" from the student's major. Departments would be permitted to offer new courses for two or three years without prior approval, and each department was asked to make a review of its objectives and course offerings every five years. To make it easier for students to design their own majors, the Council on Educational Development would be given the authority to approve such student-designed majors.

The committee made several suggestions designed to improve the quality of teaching. Among these was a proposal for the development of more specific criteria or "model standards" for the evaluation of teaching and its role in promotion and tenure decisions. The creation of a center for creative teaching and learning in the university was proposed. More careful and professional training and use of teaching assistants was called for. Furthermore, departments were urged to offer more small classes, and it was recommended that each freshman have at least two seminar courses.

Several recommendations—for more professional counselors, for student counselors, for more attention by departments to counseling—were made as part of an overall attempt to improve the quality of academic counseling. In addition, the appointment of a campus grievance officer, or ombudsman, was proposed.

The committee proposed that a study of the grading system be undertaken and urged certain revisions in examination procedures. Key among these proposals were that a two-day period be provided between the end of classes and the beginning of examinations and that students be given an opportunity to discuss graded examinations with the faculty member. The committee also urged that faculty members be encouraged to construct examinations "carefully and imaginatively" (UCLA, p. 27). The report also made several proposals regarding graduate study which are beyond the concern of this review.

**Disposition**   The report was submitted to the Academic Senate in November, 1967, and was turned over to a special steering committee. This group referred to various standing committees proposals requiring senate action, and in early 1969, most of the proposals had not been reported out of these committees. While some departments had taken some steps which the committee had recommended, the principal achievement, by early 1969, was the establishment of the Council on Educational Development. Basically, the UCLA report presented a number of ideas which would require further development by other groups. They were presented to the Academic Senate, which could do little with them until someone had developed the ideas more fully. Various departments and other groups have been developing some of these, but overall the report appears not to have generated much university-wide action.

# Part Two
# Discussion of Proposals

# 12. Classroom Teaching

The quality of teaching has been a recurring and frequently contentious issue on many campuses in recent years. Failure to rehire an untenured faculty member who was reputed to be a "great teacher"—presumably because he had failed to publish—has stirred more than one campus into protest and strike. The expressions "publish or perish" and "the flight from teaching" have become part of the language. The basic issues implicit in these clichés loomed large in the decision to undertake several of the studies reviewed here, and virtually all the reports referred to teaching. Even those which did not explicitly state it to be a problem did so implicitly by making suggestions for strengthening and improving it.

That teaching, in the best sense of the word, goes on as a part of the academic advising process, in student-teacher collaboration in research, in informal meetings over coffee or beer, and in many other sorts of encounters would be denied by few. However, the reports themselves generally treat these matters separately from classroom teaching, and they are left for discussion later on. Specifically, this chapter is concerned with three dimensions of classroom teaching which are identified in virtually all the studies: the quality of teaching and the professor's concern with it, the widespread use of teaching assistants, and the size of classes.

**THE PROFESSOR AND TEACHING** Most of the studies recognize that today's professor has many demands placed upon him to do things other than teach. (That many of these demands are self-imposed does not alter the fact of their existence.) Whatever may have been the case in some idyllic (and probably mythical) past, teaching is not now the only thing, or even the most important thing, that most professors do. As one committee put part of the problem:

The system of rewards and punishments which operates both within and without the University tends, on the whole, to encourage attention to scholarship and publications. . . . The increasing availability of funds for research in many areas further adds to its attractions. . . . What might be called "natural" forces have, in recent years, tended to make it too easy to accept a secondary position for excellence in teaching relative to excellence in research (NH, p. 38).

In addition to research of one sort or another and publication, most professors are ever more heavily involved in the administration of their institutions. The reports reviewed here, for example, represent tens of thousands of man-hours of professorial time. The many accounts of the recent crises at Berkeley, Columbia, Harvard, and elsewhere have documented the tremendous amount of time spent by faculty members in trying to bring about settlements, but even before these outbreaks, the growing complexity of normal university operations had been consuming more and more of faculty members' time and attention. As the Swarthmore report observed:

In each of the last two years twenty-two standing committees have taken up the time of 184 members. Since these assignments are made from a full-time faculty of less than 120 persons, many of whom are new and thus not subject to committee assignments . . . the burden of committee work is likely to be heavy (Sw., p. 241).

Whether as a result of research, writing, consulting, or governing the university, the modern professor—especially in the big-time universities and in what David Riesman has called the "Avis universities"—is rarely a full-time teacher, and quite commonly teaching is a relatively small part of what he does. Furthermore, the demands of committee chairmen, research assistants, publishers, or clients are generally much more obvious and unremitting, at least in the short run, than the needs of the professor's classes. Consequently, it is not surprising that the professor perhaps devotes less than a desirable amount of attention to how good his teaching is.

The quality of teaching would undoubtedly be an issue even if so much of the professor's time and atttention were not diverted to other activities, and many of the studies go on to discuss the issue in terms of the processes of teaching and the role of the teacher in those processes. In the classroom, of course, this distinction is never as sharp as is suggested here, but a hoped-for clarity of discussion leads to the separation.

**Teaching Processes**   For most faculty members, university teaching is basically lecturing. Since the lecture is most generally a way of "transmitting information (whether an orderly structure of facts, of theorems, or of theoretical interpretation) which the student must *know* in order to comprehend the subject" (Tor., p. 10), its widespread use suggests a definition of higher education as the transmitting of information. The Toronto (chap. 2), Stanford (vol. VIII), and Berkeley (chap. 3) committees gave over significant portions of their reports to the idea that the lecture is not the only way to teach (though the Berkeley committee stated quite candidly that it did "not envisage a sudden break with the tradition of lecturing at Berkeley"). Another committee felt it necessary to point out to its colleagues that ". . . research and creativity in teaching and learning cannot be left to the Graduate School of Education alone; by their very nature they are an all-University concern" (UCLA, p. 10), while another stated that ". . . we do not believe that we can continue to ignore the processes of teaching and learning, no matter what tradition may dictate" (NH, p. 47). One may think it strange that teachers would have to be admonished in these ways, but it is quite clear that the lecture—sometimes accompanied by what is called "discussion" but is really questions and answers, with the professor on one end of the exchange—dominates university classrooms. Nor, as the reports suggest, has a search for alternatives seemed of much importance to most professors.

**The Role of the Teacher**   The widespread use of the lecture may simply establish that those responsible for American higher education do, indeed, see its essential function as the transmission of information. It is also possible that lecturing is so popular because the teacher as lecturer is able to put and keep a distance between himself and the students. If the teacher sees himself simply in the role of transmitter of information, he may be able to ignore the question of the effect which he, as a man, has on the students. That this is only an illusory escape is suggested in several of the studies:

The good teacher displays his commitment to teaching by his conduct in the classroom. He reveals, in any number of ways, his respect for the course, no matter how elementary, and for the student, no matter how ordinary. By his manner, the teacher communicates how he feels about what he is doing. If he does not think it worthy of his best effort, neither will his students—and they will resent both the course and the man who has conducted it (MS, p. 24).

It is our function to teach [our students] how to think. But this is not divorced from morality. There is honesty in the life of the intellect and there is dishonesty. We should try to help our students be intellectually honest. *We do this in every contact with them, by the example we set.* This is the best service we can render to them or to mankind. Intellectual integrity is not a thing apart from training in the use of the mind. It is its very essence (Sw., p. 37, italics supplied).

And if all of scholarship—our research, our publication and our teaching— is justified, as it should be, by its devotion to humane ends, no defect of humane consideration is acceptable in our transactions with students. The image of the teacher will be no trivial part of what the world is or could be in the student's mind. It will influence the student's judgment—toward hope or cynicism—regarding the educability of man and the power of scholarship to solve human problems; it will be a part of his final attitude toward the University itself (Berk., pp. 39–40).

These are all rather strong words. However, if the Berkeley committee is correct in suggesting that the student's "image of the teacher" is an important part of his "final attitude toward the University itself," the several admonitions are neither too strong nor too soon given. The evidence is fairly overwhelming that a great many students have a generally unfavorable attitude toward alma mater. Nor will a realistic assessment of the evidence permit attribution of the dissatisfaction only to such things as the war in Vietnam or the racial crisis.

In short, the basic issue is how the professor views himself in his role as a teacher and how he is viewed by his colleagues and the administration. Part of the problem is the extent to which other activities—not entirely compatible with teaching—are permitted to consume the professor's time. Another dimension is the extent to which professors are concerned with, and give attention to, teaching as a process. The professionalization of higher education has meant that many professors see themselves primarily as writers, biologists, economists, or whatever. In such roles, the processes of teaching and learning are not often of great concern. Finally, there is the awesome conflict between the teacher viewing himself as basically a transmitter of information and the student viewing him as "no trivial part of what the world is or could be."

**Rewards for Teaching** In general, the studies seek to ensure the quality of classroom teaching by giving greater rewards for good teaching. Most of the studies focus on the need to make the quality of the professor's teaching more readily observable to those who make crucial decisions about his status and emoluments. More specifically, the reports are concerned with ways to evaluate teaching, since there is a general recognition that rewards for teaching performance must be based on prior evaluation.

Perhaps the most comprehensive proposal for evaluation is contained in the Berkeley report, which called for "a formal dossier on the teaching performance of the candidate [for tenure]." This dossier would include

... all significant tangible evidence, such as course materials and plans, syllabi, study guides, examinations, and textbooks written by the candidate. It should also include written reports by colleagues, evaluating the candidate's classroom performance *on the basis of classroom visitations,* and a statement by the candidate describing the rationale of his teaching efforts (Berk., p. 44, italics supplied).

This group also recommended that another committee design and administer "an experimental student evaluation of all undergraduate courses ... as the basis for later faculty consideration of a permanent system of student evaluation" (Berk., pp. 59–60).

The Berkeley group was the only one specifically to call for the use of classroom "inspection" of teaching performance. Since actual observation of performance is probably a very good way of judging it, the failure of other committees to propose such observation is testimony to the power of the shibboleths of academic freedom and the sanctity of the classroom. As the Toronto report put it:

It rarely occurs to an established academic person that there is any need to defend the view that his lectures should not be subject to inspection by his colleagues or superiors. Yet this position may well be questioned by the public, insofar as the public is unfamiliar with the ethos of the university, and even by the students, under considerable provocation (Tor., pp. 46–47).

The Toronto group did not, however, suggest a response to such questioning beyond "inspection of a beginning member of the profession, in his first year or two of full-time university teaching." Indeed, the final faculty action on the committee's recommendation, on the Berkeley committee's very specific call for it, was left simply as one of several things which "reviewers have found useful in evaluating teaching" (Berk., p. 240).

Most of the studies called for the use of student appraisals of individual teaching performance, and Swarthmore also asked for evaluation by graduates and by outside examiners (a part of the Swarthmore honors program). However, only New Hampshire and Duke specifically called for the use of these in tenure and promotion decisions.[1] In most cases, it is suggested that appraisals go to the individual instructor, who, if he wishes, may pass them on to his academic superior.

While every group called for consideration of teaching in decisions about promotions and tenure, it is significant that most of these calls were simply reaffirmations of existing institutional policy. The specific proposals made in the reports came down, in the last analysis, to little more than exhortation, or the "teacher-of-the-year" awards proposed at Duke and Michigan State. As we wrote in the New Hampshire report, "Many faculty members are equally loud in their demands for the reward of good teaching and in their insistence that teaching performance cannot be measured. They cannot have it both ways" (NH, p. 45). From the evidence of the several reports it seems that they have not given up trying. Everyone wants teaching to be rewarded, but except for the Berkeley committee, whose recommendations were, as noted, much watered down in final action by the faculty, no one is very specific about how teaching might be evaluated or about how the results of such evaluation might be used in deciding upon rewards.

We are doubtful that any routine devices of this sort will contribute very much to doing what needs to be done. What is important is that there be a formal procedure, not necessarily that it be reduced to or contain a large element of routine procedure. What is needed above all is Faculty insistence that departments not be permitted to be negligent in weighing teaching

---

[1] Two years after the recommendation by the New Hampshire committee, no action had been taken. The Duke proposal was included in an appendix to the committee report and was not a formal recommendation to the faculty or the administration.

ability in recommending promotions and appointments. The deans are now in a position to exercise their influence in appointments and promotions to positions carrying tenure. They should make it clear to chairmen that they expect teaching ability to be weighed also in recommendations for appointments and promotions below tenure rank. We look on this not as an encroachment on the rightful powers and responsibilities of chairmen, but as a reserve power to prevent the possibility of their actions encroaching on the rights of the academic community (Tor., p. 48).

This statement by the Toronto committee is forthright, but does not really face up to the situation described in the Duke report:

The data available suggest that departmental chairmen do have ways of evaluating the teaching of their faculty members, but that these ways might best be described as being based on informally gathered hearsay or on the presumption that a faculty member's teaching is satisfactory unless negative comment is received from students (Duke, p. J15).

The problem which the studies ultimately fail to resolve is that of what the place of teaching is in all that the professor does. As the Wesleyan study pointed out:

In general it can be said that an outstanding teacher or a total failure can be identified and that either of these judgments (especially the latter) will count heavily in decisions on reappointment or tenure. If a man is obviously doing a steady and competent job, the case for promotion and tenure is generally made on other grounds (Wes., I, p. 8).

Others are perhaps less sanguine:

We find there is widespread belief, among faculty and students, that appointments and promotions are made primarily or entirely on the basis of research and publication (or, in the case of very junior people, on the basis of presumed aptitude for research and publication), with teaching ability left out of the picture. We know that this is an overstatement, but we think there is enough truth in it to merit some attention (Tor., p. 43).

Rewards flow more easily to achievements measured solely by scholarly productivity and conscientious teachers become seriously discouraged (MS, p. 22).

Whether the extreme cases of poor (or good) teaching are or are not identified may be left as moot. The important point of the foregoing is that the *professor* is generally evaluated on grounds other than teaching and that, for the most part, these other grounds turn out to be publication.

All the studies wrestled with the question of whether research and, by implication, consulting and administration are compatible with teaching, and the universal conclusion is that they are. The Berkeley committee stated that ". . . teaching and researching in a University setting do not conflict but support each other. There is, of course, a sense in which they are activities which compete for the professor's limited time, and a proper balance should be maintained between them" (Berk., p. 42). The Toronto committee asserted that ". . . the best teachers are usually productive scholars, or at least that a university which did not have a high proportion of scholars on its staff would not be one in which good university teaching would flourish" (Tor., p. 43).

While there is some obeisance in the direction of excellent teachers who do not publish, the groups generally concluded that research or scholarship (which are never really defined) is a necessary concomitant of good teaching. For the most part, this is taken as a matter of faith. No one, for example, attempted to assess the publication activity of "good" teachers. It is simply assumed that with a few possible exceptions, good teachers are researchers and published writers. It is recognized that ". . . however complementary excellence in scholarship and excellence in teaching may be, they are not identical: and that the claims of scholarly research and undergraduate teaching on the working hours of the professor may pull in opposite directions" (Tor., p. 43). And thus the reports are always drawn back to the solution of greater rewards for teaching as the only apparent way out of the dilemma.

**TEACHING ASSISTANTS**  Tremendous increases in enrollments, the diversion of professors into activities other than teaching, and the almost universal desire for small classes (to be discussed below) have meant that more and more of the teaching of undergraduates is done by teaching assistants in all but the very smallest undergraduate colleges.[2] That these young people are not always appropriate substitutes for experienced professors is suggested by the statements that "The

[2] At Berkeley in 1965, "31 percent of the total number of classes were sections regularly taught by Teaching Assistants or were laboratories in which supervision is usually in their hands. Of the lower division classes, 41 percent were of this kind" (Berk., p. 175).

degree to which graduate students in the various departments at Duke receive any such supervision or training [in teaching] varies from considerable to none at all with the mode at very little" (Duke, p. J14) and that "too many teaching assistants have not taught well enough, and too many have not profited sufficiently from the experience" (Berk., p. 176). The problem, then, is quite simply that if classes are not to be gigantic assemblies, the use of teaching assistants becomes essential, and because of a lack of training and perhaps of motivation, the quality of their teaching is, on the whole, not good. Furthermore, the quality of the teaching of the teaching assistant is undoubtedly affected by the fact that, like the professor, he has other demands on his time. He is normally engaged in graduate course work or preparation of a dissertation, and even if he is fortunate enough to have a working wife, he is undoubtedly concerned with how to survive on the miserable stipend he receives. Thus his teaching may not have his undivided or enthusiastic attention. As the Berkeley report put it, "While the faculty member may find himself divided between the demands of research and teaching, the teaching assistant is torn by them" (Berk., p. 177).

Several of the study groups proposed arrangements for giving prospective teachers some training in teaching. For example, at Duke it was proposed that

. . . it be a university policy that graduate student education at Duke include some training in teaching, at least for those graduate students who plan to spend any portion of their time in teaching. Such training should include apprenticeship, supervision, evaluation, and feedback to the graduate students (Duke, p. J14).

The Berkeley study recommended that:

Frequent regular meetings between professors and Teaching Assistants, including graduate teaching colloquia or teaching seminars where appropriate to the discipline, should be a part of the regular program in each department, and should be counted as teaching credit of faculty and course or service credits of students (Berk., p. 182).

Most of the studies made similar recommendations, but at the time of this writing, little formal action had been taken on any of them. Perhaps the fundamental issue is reflected in the following discussion taken from the Toronto report:

As long as teaching assistants are regarded merely as an expedient to prevent the teaching load of full-time staff from becoming intolerable, any claim they in turn make on the time and attention of the professors to whom they are assigned is apt to be resented. It is still not unknown for a professor to say that teaching assistants are more trouble than they are worth, since it takes as long to show them what to do and to supervise their doing it as to do it oneself. . . .

To the extent that this attitude still prevails what is needed above all is a recognition that teaching assistants are here to stay and a willingness to make their work a positive contribution to undergraduate teaching rather than treating them as a necessary evil (Tor., p. 51).

In their analyses of the problem, the studies made it abundantly clear that any effort to urge those planning to join university faculties to become concerned with, and informed about, classroom teaching would be useful. Even more useful will be actual help in developing teaching skills. A recent study by Ann M. Heiss (1969) documents the need much more fully than the reports reviewed here. Perhaps it will occasion rather more response than the several studies have.

**SMALL CLASSES** The studies make it clear that most faculty members (and probably most students) have it as an article of faith that small classes are, as a general proposition, good. In one way or another, virtually all the studies discuss the need for more small classes, although they display a considerable degree of tentativeness about why this need exists. In general, the analyses seem to reflect feelings about the desirability of "communication between student and teacher" (NH, p. 42), about the conclusion that "many students seem to be lost in the large class situation" (UCLA, p. 12), or about the fact that there is a need to provide an "opportunity for dialogue" (Berk., p. 48). That these things are desirable (or undesirable) and that small classes bring them about (or eliminate them) is about as far as most of the analyses go.

The Duke report buttresses its recommendations for small classes with the argument that the anonymity of the student in a large class has a direct effect on his response to the educational system:

Apparently the freshman condition of being a stranger changes very little in respect to what should be a primary educational relationship during the undergraduate years. Most seniors at Duke, when trying to assemble a number of recommendations for jobs or graduate school, come to the inescapable realization that much of their formal education has been conducted anonymously . . . [and] to many students a professor is primarily a man who lectures to them and grades them. If the only tangible evidence a student has of a professor's awareness and approval of him is his grade, it is not surprising that some students work largely for grades, while others, seeing such impersonal approval as not worth the effort, decide not to bother working (Duke, p. 7).

The Duke study also suggests certain positive educational values arising from student involvement in smaller classes:

Proficiency in speaking is important in and after college. If every student must take some classes in which the format, size, and instructor all compel him to take a position and defend it orally, and in which they encourage him to consider the positions of his fellow students and professors, he should develop the skill, assurance and mental agility to speak under stress. Engaging in intellectual discussion with his fellow students in class will encourage him to continue intellectual discussion beyond the classroom, and he should come to rely less on professors and assigned work, and more on himself and his environment for his education. By engaging in direct discussion with his professor, a student can discover more meaningfully than in a lecture his professor's approach to problems, his insight into his subject, and the quality of his mind. The student may come to know the professor as a person, not simply to hear his words, and so be drawn into the life of the scholarly community (Duke, p. 23).

One might respond to the foregoing by suggesting that it is less a defense of small classes than an attack on the lecture. The Harvard Business School, for example, has long been highly successful in compelling a student "to take a position and defend it orally," encouraging him "to consider the positions of his fellow students and professors," and developing "the skill, assurance and mental agility to speak under stress." And the Harvard Business School has done this in classes which quite typically include 100 or more students. This has been possible because the faculty has seen its role as one of helping students to develop analytical skills rather than one of transmitting information.[3] In its discussion of class

---

[3] I do not intend to suggest that methods of classroom teaching developed at the Harvard Business School are universally applicable. They are particularly suited to that school's curriculum and objectives. Furthermore, it is not clear that they particularly achieve the other objective of allowing the student to come to "know the professor as a person." The point is simply that a small class is not a necessary condition for drawing students into intellectual exchanges.

size, the Toronto study questions whether the use of the class—whatever its size—is not an anachronistic means of transmitting information in this age of Xerox, television, and computers. The Toronto group makes the point that small classes are not necessarily better than large ones if their purpose is simply that of the large lecture:

If, as we have found, much of the lecturing in the Faculty consists mainly of the transmission of information from lecturer to student, it is not surprising that some tutorials have come to be used primarily to ensure that students have received and absorbed the information so transmitted [and when] given by someone other than the lecturer himself, there has been an understandable tendency for them to become additional miniature lectures or monologues by the instructor . . . (Tor., p. 32).

The Toronto study suggests that the need for small classes arises because the class should be devoted not to transmitting information but to permitting students to "see how the more experienced mind of the professor operates on the subject-matter of a particular discipline—how he examines it critically, [analyzes] it, finds unapparent relations between different things in it, and so on . . ." (Tor., pp. 31–32).

Virtually all the studies made proposals about small classes, ranging from rather general policy proposals to very specific rules. The general proposal is illustrated by that made by the Berkeley group:

It should be the policy of the administration and faculty to increase the opportunity of all students for learning based on dialogue and on cooperative student self-instruction, by decreasing the proportion of lecture courses in favor of discussion sections, small classes, seminars, tutorials, preceptorials and similar teaching arrangements (Berk., p. 50).

Whether because of the general nature of this proposal or because of some other factor, the response of the Berkeley senate to it was to place it on file.

At Michigan State, the committee urged the central university administration to give "top priority in the allocation of new positions for undergraduate teaching" to departments with very large enrollments. It also urged "steps . . . to insure . . . increased participation of regular faculty in teaching and in directing the large enrollment courses" (MS, p. 30). The Educational Development

Program (manned by part of the provost's staff) had been giving major attention to helping individuals and departments achieve some greater measure of small group instruction, and the study committee urged that this be continued.

At New Hampshire, we urged that every student in the university be given the opportunity to participate in a class of no more than 10 students at least once in each of his four years. To implement this, it was recommended that each department organize "at least one course normally taken by many students as a part of General Education requirements or as an elective, so that it can be handled on a small group basis" (NH, p. 42). We recommended that each department be required to report its plans and begin implementation in September, 1967, but by mid-1969 no action had been taken.

A freshman seminar program was proposed at New Hampshire, and the Stanford committee called for continued expansion of the program already in existence there. In both cases, an important objective was to encourage departures from the rather stereotyped content of most departmental introductory courses, but they were also intended to give freshmen the experience of participation in a small class. The limitation of 20 students in the modes-of-thought courses at Brown was directed toward the same end.

The recommendations of the Toronto committee were more specific and all-embracing. They recommended that in all classes in which two or three lectures per week were given, the number of lectures be reduced to one per week and one tutorial per week. They would further require that tutorials include from five to ten students (Tor., p. 20). At the time of this writing, these proposals had not been implemented.

By far the most far-reaching proposals were those made by the Duke committee. Each freshman and each sophomore would participate in a seminar in one semester or in a preceptorial, discussion section, or tutorial during both semesters. Juniors and seniors would take seminars or do independent study equivalent to at least two courses (Duke, p. 30). Their recommendations would ensure that all students had a variety of learning experience and that much of their formal course work would be done independently or in small groups. The recommendations were accepted by the Duke faculty, and the proposals were phased in beginning in September, 1969.

If one accepts, as all the studies do, that small classes are an important element in achieving more effective teaching and learning, one must face their very high cost. Even if faculty members were to spend more time teaching, any large-scale subdivision of classes would require increases in faculty and therefore more money. Some offsets are available: the Toronto proposal for eliminating a certain number of the meetings of each course, the New Hampshire proposal for replacing some middle-sized classes with very large ones, and Duke's reduction in the number of courses normally taken by each student. Ultimately, however, the arithmetic of the situation is inexorable. Mass higher education cannot become intimate without substantial increases in cost.

**CONCLUSION**  On the whole, the several reports candidly pointed to the often routine and sometimes deplorable quality of the teaching done by many college and university professors. They make it quite clear that the teaching assistant needs more and better training and a more dignified status, although their proposals for achieving either of these ends have not been enthusiastically received. They all display a strong conviction that students must be gotten out of some of their large classes, but they offer little guidance on how small learning groups are to be staffed. One obviously helpful step would be for each faculty member to spend more time teaching, but this would surely impinge on various other professional activities. Thus the studies all come back to greater rewards as the only apparent way to improve the quality of teaching. But since none of the studies has proposed really effective ways for evaluating teaching, one may wonder how the rewards can match those offered under the reward system of the scholarly guilds described by Riesman and Jencks (1968) and Caplow and McGee (1965). More than one Duke faculty member wondered whether the untenured faculty member would really give his time and effort to provide "varieties of learning experience" when he knows that his promotion and his mobility ultimately depend on publication. In only slightly different forms, this question is asked on every campus.

# 13. Advising

The impersonality of the campus has been a principal element in student complaints of recent years. Large numbers of students complain that they can spend four years in a college without even getting to know a faculty member. The IBM card has become the symbol of the bureaucratized campus, just as the growing phenomenon of T groups and related activities seems to be a reaction against it. Impersonality, of course, has been widely observed as a characteristic of contemporary American life, and many of the factors which may give rise to it are external to the university. However, among the important causes of impersonality in the university are large size and the routinization and superficiality of relationships which seem to accompany it. In a large institution the need for personal relationships—especially those which cross status barriers—becomes hard to satisfy, and channels of necessary communication become difficult to keep open. Both of these factors are at the core of the academic advising problem with which most students deal.[1]

**THE NATURE OF THE PROBLEM** All the colleges and universities included in this study had advising systems of some sort which shared a number of objectives. For one thing, the systems were intended to provide students with information about courses and programs available and requirements to be met. Largely inseparable from the information function was a policing function, for the requirement that each student "discuss his program with his adviser" was intended to ensure that students did what they were supposed to do. Finally, the systems attempted

---

[1] On some campuses, academic advising is referred to as "counseling." I have not used the latter term here because it so often implies professional psychological assistance—a matter which only the Stanford study refers to in any major way.

to ensure that each student had a faculty member to whom he could go for advice about courses, program selection, or career choices and (at least as students generally see it) to whom he could talk in an informal fashion.

Each of the studies also stated, in one way or another, that advising was a major problem, and all reviewed much the same reasons for the failure of the system to work effectively. The overriding problem is that most faculty members do not like to do the job and, in general, do not do it well. As the Stanford study put it, "The faculty are, on the whole, indifferent to advising; the advising they give is generally indifferent in quality . . . (Stan., V, p. 12). There are a number of reasons for this indifference. For one thing, it is never entirely clear just what advising is. The New Hampshire committee stated:

The *need* for advising arises from a whole spectrum of situations ranging from course selection, through difficulties in adjusting to university life and in career selection, to problems rooted in personality disorders (NH, p. 27).

It went on to suggest that there is no single way to meet all these needs, a fact which may be at the root of much faculty indifference. Few faculty members care to see themselves as a cog in the bureaucratic machinery—as mere initialers of student course schedules and as policemen. Most faculty members also have a real and undoubtedly healthy reluctance toward becoming involved with students' emotional problems. Ideally, the faculty adviser's role would be structured so as to rule out one or both of these aspects. Unfortunately, one can rarely predict the course of any encounter between faculty adviser and student advisee. A ritual card signing might lead to a conversation which would involve the student in a meaningful review of his situation and plans. A discussion about course selection or about graduate school might unexpectedly reveal a student's deep-seated emotional problems. The possibility that such situations might arise no doubt has much to do with the "indifference" of faculty members.

A second problem concerns the amount of time that advising can consume. As the Michigan State committee wrote, "It is simply not possible [for one professor] to advise in any effective way 70 to 100 students . . ." (MS, p. 105). Perhaps few of the other universities and colleges represented here must ask professors to deal with so many students, but one-half or even one-third of that number would still involve a great deal of time. This situation is partly a result of the fact that faculty membership has not always expanded so rapidly as student enrollment. More generally it results from the factors discussed in the previous chapter: Among all the things that the contemporary professor is expected and expects to do, advising students does not loom large.

A further problem has, in a sense, been created by the changes recommended in the studies. The Swarthmore study, for example, admitted that ". . . the need for advising will be increased rather than diminished, by some of the curricular changes we are recommending" (Sw., p. 194). Most of the studies recommended some lessening of the requirements in their general education programs, and several would permit students to design their own majors. Both of these moves toward greater freedom for students involve a responsibility to ensure that students who wish it have ready access to sound advice. A prescribed curriculum is obviously a sort of mass advising, and since most of the reports propose moves away from prescribed curricula, the need for a more effective advising system is clear.

In this same connection, some of the reports referred to the fact that faculty advisers frequently do not know enough about courses and programs available or about requirements to give students good advice even if they wanted to take the necessary time. A cynic at Toronto observed that ". . . the one uniform test imposed on all students . . . is their obligation to find their way through the [catalogue] and for that reason it should not be made any more easily comprehensible" (Tor., p. 119). This would apply to virtually any college catalogue, and generally they are as baffling to faculty members as they are to students.

Finally, there is the question of student-faculty contact. The Berkeley report noted that students say ". . . they would like to discuss meaningful topics with faculty members, but they feel that the short and obligatory appointment at the beginning of each semester does not furnish an opportunity conducive to informal discussion" (Berk., p. 81).

Thus the advising system tends to fail both as a channel of information and as a basis for significant contact between students and faculty members.

**SUGGESTED**
**CHANGES**

The need for a better information flow can be met in large part by the publication of more timely, more clear, and more informative descriptions of courses, programs, and requirements. Several of the reports made recommendations toward that end. The information problem can also be partly handled by organizing a group of persons whose job it is to be informed. Michigan State, for example, proposed the establishment of an advisement center in each of its colleges. The committee suggested that:

So long as the college advisement center is staffed by advisers thoroughly acquainted with University, and especially college requirements and patterns of study, and so long as it has available to it liaison faculty members in each of the departments of the college to whom it can turn when necessary, then the advisement center can play an important role in improving the quality of academic counsel available to undergraduate students (MS, p. 107).

Several of the studies recommended the creation or strengthening of such groups.

While these several approaches may deal effectively with the information aspect of academic advising, they do nothing to further opportunities for faculty-student interaction. The problem here is essentially a matter of priorities and motivation—both for the individual faculty member and for the institution. Only Stanford's report directly tackled the matter of individual motivation. That report proposed that faculty members serving as advisers to 15 or more freshmen receive extra compensation up to $500 per year and that those serving as advisers to 15 or more upperclassmen be provided with extra research assistance. In addition, the Stanford committee recommended that performance as an adviser be specifically considered in promotion and tenure decisions.

Even with some resolution of the motivation question, the problem of numbers would remain. The colleges and universities included here have faculty-student ratios ranging between 1 to 8 or 9 and 1 to 15 or 16. Certainly most faculty members should be able to spend a reasonable amount of time with each of 8 or 9 students, and while 15 or 16 may be more difficult, it is not an impossible number. However, it is well known that these overall ratios are relatively meaningless in terms of individual subunits in the university. The teacher-student ratio is typically very much higher in some departments and schools than in others. Furthermore, not all faculty members are available for general advising duties. Some teach only graduate students, some are research professors, some are in nonteaching institutes, and so on. Thus in many parts of the university it is simply impossible to have a reasonably small number of students assigned to a faculty adviser. Consequently, while the advising system is the traditional locus of faculty-student contact, many of the studies looked to other points in the overall environment for such contact. As the Swarthmore study put it:

In the last analysis, faculty-student relations cannot stand or fall by the academic advising system . . . a healthy and mutually enriching interaction depends on many points of contact: If a student can become friendly with a few faculty members whom he has come to know in the classroom or through a mutual concern for peace or poetry or basketball, or in occasional accidental encounters and philosophical disputes in the dining halls, then he ought to feel that there is someone he can turn to for academic counsel, as well as for personal and vocational counsel, when he is so minded (Sw., p. 197).

As the Swarthmore report states in the passage just quoted, there are several points in the total academic environment where mutually rewarding interactions between faculty members and students can take place. Most of the studies identified the classroom or laboratory as a central point for contact between students and faculty and consequently made the proposals for small classes described in the preceding chapter. There appears to be a widespread feeling that relationships which grow out of mutual interests in a subject and joint efforts to master a subject are most likely to become effective relationships. This conclusion is one of the principal reasons for the attraction of small classes in the freshman year and for the proposal at Stanford and New Hampshire, for example, that the teachers of freshman seminars also be designated as the advisers of the students in the seminars.

Several of the committees also saw residences as a basis for establishing student-faculty relationships. Michigan State and Wesleyan—and, to a lesser extent, Toronto—had already combined teaching with residence through their several residential colleges. Both urged expansion of these arrangements. New Hampshire proposed a number of experimental approaches to associating faculty members with student residences. At Duke, a special committee was, at the time of this writing, investigating the question of bringing academic activities into the residences. UCLA proposed the establishment of instructional-residential centers. While the Stanford study was under way, a decision was made to carry on some instruction in dormitories, and the activity is being expanded.

"Community" has become a sadly overworked word on many campuses in recent years. On the other hand, an absence of community appears to be behind proposals to bring together the academic and nonacademic aspects of university life. These proposals for residential-educational groupings were not conceived of by the committees in terms of academic advising only. Broadly speaking, they were intended to overcome some of the disadvantages of large size and intellectual isolation. But they were also intended to provide a more effective basis for establishing relationships between students and faculty members and between students and students, and perhaps between faculty members, too. The widespread disappearance of such relationships, as most American campuses have grown larger and more diverse, has simultaneously created the need for and demonstrated the inadequacies of formal, bureaucratized advising systems.

# 14. Curriculum: General Education

In reading this chapter and the one that follows, it is particularly important to remember that this study is based mainly on "regular" four-year undergraduate programs of colleges and universities and has been concerned almost exclusively with the regular, overall curricula of those institutions. Many curricular experiments and innovations go on in institutions not represented here, especially the avowedly experimental ones—Antioch, Hampshire, Montieth, Sarah Lawrence, and the like. There is also some innovation and experimentation going on in small experimental units within larger institutions—the Tussman Program at Berkeley and Justin Morrill College at Michigan State, for example—but these latter have received only marginal, if any, attention in the reports being reviewed, and that attention is concerned mostly with organizational matters. Thus, what follows should not be read as an overall review of current curricular developments in American higher education. On the other hand, it is a fact that the overwhelming majority of students are enrolled in the regular parts of regular four-year institutions and that the overwhelming majority of faculty members do teach in these institutions. The basis for this discussion may not be representative, but it is surely typical.

During the past hundred or so years, American curricular development has, in at least two aspects, exhibited a considerable degree of schizophrenia. One of these aspects involves the conflict between largely prescribed curricula and essentially free electives —between the faculty's selection of what is essential from among the ever-expanding realm of things to study and the student's own selection, with or without the counsel and approval of a faculty member. The other aspect is the conflict between general education and specialization—between the concept of the "well-rounded" man and that of the highly trained engineer, psychologist, or what-

**169**

ever. These two levels are not always separate and distinct. General education in its organized, as opposed to its philosophical, sense has generally involved some degree of prescription—for example, "Every educated person must have some understanding of the Western cultural heritage, and therefore all students must take a course in contemporary civilization." Specialization as an element in American higher education got a major boost from Eliot at Harvard in the 1880s, and Eliot coupled specialization with the introduction of the free-elective idea. Nevertheless, in more recent times, as the amount of knowledge involved in even a modest command of a particular subject has increased, so has the degree of prescription involved in studying that subject.[1]

While each of the institutions included in this review had its own curriculum, the basic structure of the several curricula was much the same in all of them when the committees began their work. There was some sort of general education program which involved varying degrees of prescription. The student was also required to major or concentrate in one subject or area, with the extent of the concentration and degree of prescription involved varying in different fields. On the whole, the studies have little to say about the basic nature of the major or concentration,[2] but all devoted much attention to the question of general education. As the following review of changes proposed by the studies will indicate, the common element is some movement in the direction of permitting students to design their own general education programs.

**GENERAL EDUCATION**  General education programs have traditionally taken one of two forms: structured programs made up of specially designed core courses not confined to a single discipline—"contemporary civilization," for example—or a distribution or breadth requirement built largely on the regular departmental course offerings—usually

---

[1] The history of these developments until about 1920 has been fully recounted by Lawrence R. Vesey in *The Emergence of the American University* (The University of Chicago Press, Chicago, 1965). Frederick Rudolph, in *The American College and University* (Vintage Books, New York, 1965, especially chaps. 21 and 22), brings the story up to about 1960. The triumph of specialization is portrayed in Christopher Jencks and David Riesman, *The Academic Revolution,* Doubleday & Company, Inc., Garden City, N.Y., 1968, chap. 12.

[2] Brown and Swarthmore are exceptions. The Swarthmore study devoted a great deal of attention to the honors program, its unique form of concentration. The Brown report discussed the nature of concentration at some length. These and other matters relating to concentration are discussed in the next chapter.

at the introductory level.[3] Among the institutions included in this study only Columbia and Michigan State had structured programs with specially designed general education courses. (At Michigan State the courses have been taught by special departments in a special college — University College — in which all entering students enrolled.) All the others had a distribution requirement as the basis for their general education programs, though there are variations, such as New Hampshire's and Stanford's combination of a required course — Introduction to Contemporary Civilization — with distribution. Under the typical distribution requirement, the student took a certain number of courses in the traditional divisions of the curriculum — the humanities, the social sciences, and the natural sciences — plus a course in English composition and a foreign language. The makeup of the divisions, the number of courses required, and other details vary, but the foregoing are characteristic of virtually all the requirements.

**Changes in Structured Programs**  Daniel Bell stands alone in proposing an increase in the general education requirements. He would add a third semester to the two-semester sequence in comtemporary civilization and a third semester, concerned with modern and contemporary art, to the two-semester humanities sequence. The science requirement would be kept at two full years, but the focus would be narrowed to either a mathematics-physics or a mathematics-biology sequence. Beyond these, Bell proposed adding a requirement for "third-tier" courses to be taken in the senior year. These would "brake the drive toward specialization by trying to generalize [the student's] experiences in his discipline" (Bell, 1966, p. 293). Bell finally proposed elimination — except on a noncredit, remedial basis — of the requirement for a course in English composition.

In all other cases except one, the reports proposed some reduction in the number and range of courses required, and they generally recommended that substitution of advanced-level courses for introductory courses be permitted to satisfy distribution requirements. Michigan State did not propose a reduction in its general education requirements, but did suggest shifting emphasis from the

---

[3] Daniel Bell (1966, pp. 284–285) argues that distribution requirements are not general education. His criticisms have cogency, but it is true that many institutions define general education in terms of the distribution or breadth requirement. Bell's book also provides a thorough, if narrowly based, history of the general education idea, and it seems unnecessary to repeat its substance here.

specifically designed general education courses by permitting students to substitute regular departmental courses for two of the University College sequences.[4]

Only the Swarthmore study discussed replacement of its distribution requirement with a structured general education program. It rejected the idea for reasons to be reviewed later. In short, Bell's sturdy defense not withstanding, it appears that the age of the *Redbook* is rapidly drawing to a close.

**Changes in Distribution Requirements**

It is difficult to summarize changes proposed elsewhere because the details vary. Wesleyan eliminated all requirements, leaving entirely to the student the design of his own general education program. In the several cases where the distribution requirements previously had to be met from lists of prescribed courses in the natural sciences, the social sciences, and the humanities, it was generally proposed that any course in those areas be permitted to satisfy the requirement, and as noted earlier, advanced courses in a field would be permitted to serve the purpose. In the recommendations, the language requirement was almost universally a casualty, although institutional realities usually overcome educational logic at the time for action. It generally proved easier to retain the requirement than to decide what to do with members of language departments who would no longer have students to teach.[5] Only New Hampshire joined Bell in proposing to phase out freshman English, but in many other reports it was proposed that the course become more specifically a composition course and that the study of literature as such be eliminated or substantially curtailed.

On the whole, the results of the studies range from maintenance of the *status quo* to a reduction—occasionally elimination—of specific content requirements for the general education part of the student's program. At the same time, no decrease in the quantity of the student's program to be taken outside his area of specialization was proposed. In other words, the authors of most of the studies do not seem happy with either of the traditional approaches to general education, although they are unwilling to give up the idea

---

[4] As explained in the Michigan State case (pp. 81–94), the issue was concerned as much with the basically political problem of University College as with the philosophical problems of general education.

[5] Or so it was generally thought. Stanford did abandon its language requirement (although some departments substituted their own), and the enrollment in elementary language courses increased.

that part of an American college education should be general, as opposed to specialized. None of them—with the possible exception of Brown—has any very strong ideas about possible replacements.

**Changes at Brown** Brown's study committee, basically following the recommendations of students, proposed the replacement of a more or less traditional distribution requirement with the requirement that the student take at least five (not more than seven) modes-of-thought courses, preferably in the freshman year, and in any case before the junior year. These courses would be based generally upon a particular problem or issue which might well involve more than one field and would be concerned primarily with the methods, concepts, and value systems involved in attacking such a problem. That is, the courses would be directed toward considering why an area should be studied and how to study it, rather than toward mastering a particular body of material about it. It was intended that the subject matter of the courses be based on the interests of an instructor or instructors, rather than being designed by a department or prescribed by the traditions of a particular discipline. Thus the courses would rarely be offered for more than a year or two. Student interest would also be an important determinant of the life of these courses. It was also urged that such courses "not be a prerequisite for any advanced course [because] the danger exists that pressures may be placed on the course to shape its directions in order to serve the purposes of advanced students" (Br., p. 16).

None of these approaches to course design and teaching is new, of course. What is new—among the institutions studied for this report and beyond them, I believe—is their wholesale incorporation into a general education program. If fully implemented, the Brown general education program would be significantly different from either the structured programs or the distribution requirements based on departmental, discipline-based courses. The case study of the changes at Brown (pp. 107–121) suggests that it is too soon to tell whether they will be fully implemented. These changes were proposed initially by students and were accepted largely because of intense student pressure for curriculum reform. Their implementation may depend on the continuation of such pressure.

**THE COMMITTEES' ARGUMENTS** Except at Brown, most of the reports basically supported maintenance of the *status quo* or a reduction in general education requirements and used much the same arguments for doing so. In rejecting the approach to general education advocated by Daniel Bell, the Swarthmore committee argued:

One problem is to define for the institution the ends and content of "core" courses, a problem that has grown with recognition of traditions once considered exotic and with increasing emphasis on "methods of inquiry." Difficulty alone is not an insufficient reason for not attempting a general specification of objectives and methods; but widespread disagreement on these suggests there are merits in a pluralistic approach. A second set of problems lies in staffing and administration; while some faculty members find general education stimulating, at least for a time, professional demands compete with it, and variation in content in the interest of professional development conflicts with clarity of purpose (Sw., p. 60).

The Swarthmore committee was, in the foregoing passage, arguing against a structured general education program and for a distribution requirement. In arguing for a very substantial reduction in existing distribution requirements, the Stanford committee employed essentially the same arguments:

It is inevitable that a program as highly prescribed as the Stanford General Studies Program will reflect, explicitly or implicitly, judgments of differential significance that are difficult to defend. Why, for example, is it more important for a student to learn some calculus than some economics? Are we really sure that mastery of a foreign language is more important than mastery of one of the fine arts? More important to whom or to what? It is no answer to questions of this order that various requirements represent a set of political compromises among interest groups in the faculty, although that explanation probably comes closer to the truth than do more nearly principled ones. . . . The faculty of today's university, for better or for worse, consists of discipline-oriented specialists. The faculty member whom the university seeks to attract is an individualist who, while accepting the collegial responsibility of shared tasks within his discipline, nonetheless prefers to teach and learn what *he* wants to teach and learn, not what is prescribed by a committee (Stan., II, pp. 9–10).

It is interesting, in passing, to observe how those problems are sometimes rationalized. Swarthmore introduced the above-quoted discussion of the problems of a structured general education program by observing that these may especially be problems of a small college. At New Hampshire we argued that the university was too large and too heterogeneous to support an effective structured general education program, although we thought that a small liberal arts college could do so. In matters of curriculum as elsewhere, it appears, the other fellow's grass is greener.

These discussions explicitly or implicitly identify the "knowledge explosion" and the Academic Revolution as the principal roots of the problem of general education. The tremendous growth of man's knowledge apparently makes the task of sorting out that which should be broadly familiar to every degree holder extremely difficult, if not impossible. Even if it were possible, it seems that most faculty members, usually highly trained in a relatively narrow specialty and more devoted to that specialty than to education in general, would be unwilling or unable to do the sorting.

Daniel Bell refuses to accept the first of these problems as more than a difficulty, asserting, "The intellectual difficulties encountered in organizing the general education courses . . . though genuine, do not constitute any reason for eliminating these courses, but for revising them" (1966, p. 183). Bell does go on to admit that the fact "that the loyalty and allegiance of a young scholar is increasingly drawn to his department and his discipline . . . is quite serious in its implication" (1966, p. 67). While Bell is quite correct in his analysis[6]—and, incidentally, by his own admission offers little by way of solution to that problem—perhaps he does not go far enough.

The Stanford study asked, "Who is to say that some study of calculus is more important than some study of economics?" One might respond to this rhetorical question with an equally rhetorical answer: "Daniel Bell." As Martin Trow observed, "Bell nowhere argues the virtue of academic planning on a college-wide basis: the argument is the book itself" (1968). Bell does answer the Stanford question and many, many others like it, but unfortunately, Daniel Bell does not a university make—nor does any other individual —at least not since the demise of Mark Hopkins. The case studies indicate that the organizational realities of most universities would

[6] Martin Trow, in his comparison of the Bell and Muscatine reports, makes some very pointed observations about both aspects of the problem—especially about why faculties are unwilling to make the efforts which Bell demands. Trow is referring essentially to Berkeley, but his observations appear to have much wider applicability—even to Swarthmore. See "Bell, Book and Berkeley," *The American Behavioral Scientist,* May-June, 1968, pp. 43–48.

scarcely permit a group of any size to go through the process of analysis and judgment required to reach conclusions like Bell's, even if the loyalty to discipline were not overpowering.[7]

**Students**   In addition to the knowledge explosion and the Academic Revolution, most of the discussions about general education were also concerned with the "new student." Brought up in McLuhan's "global village" and prepared in post-Sputnik schools, the students seemed to many of the committees to be rather different from those most of the general education programs were planned to educate. Several of the studies pointed out that students were becoming better prepared as a result of advanced placement programs and generally upgraded secondary school course content. Furthermore, the expansion of the secondary school curriculum was taken to mean that students, as a group, had more varied academic backgrounds than students did when most of the general education programs were developed.

Better preparation meant that uniform introductory courses, inevitably designed for the typical or average student, "often seem thin or too easy" (Wes., IV, p. 6). "The diversity of student preparation and interest alone argues for greater flexibility" (MS, p. 62). Furthermore, it seemed to us at New Hampshire that if students have the ability and the necessary preparation to do advanced work in an area of interest, it would be harmful to prevent them from developing that interest at once.

Once again Daniel Bell was a sturdy dissenter, arguing (1966, pp. 124–126) that better and more diverse preparation of students is not a reason for abandoning the general education program. Indeed, he asserts that some secondary school curricular reforms have gone too far—that for some subjects, maturity as well as intelligence is a prerequisite for effective study.

In general, however, the reports indicated considerable lack of confidence that the general education programs were very well related to the needs and backgrounds of many contemporary students, and they generally proposed arrangements that would give the student more opportunity to seek out courses which would more nearly meet his perceived requirements—to get away from "general education by the registrar's office" (Stan., II, p. 8).

---

[7] This issue is discussed in detail in chap. 16.

*Knowledge about students*

Several comments on the question of adapting general education programs to the students are in order. For one thing, most of the committees admitted to knowing relatively little about their students. Virtually all the committees commented upon a lack of data about students and called for keeping and using better records about their backgrounds and progress. Even at relatively tiny Swarthmore, the committee reported that ". . . for most of the questions we asked about educational policy, hard information with which to answer them was either nonexistent or inaccessible . . ." (Sw., p. 261). The Muscatine committee at Berkeley, faced with the same lack of information, commissioned an in-depth study of one class from entrance to graduation. (Unfortunately, the results of the study were available too late to permit them to be used by the committee. Even more unfortunately, the mass of data had not been examined at all two years after the conclusion of the Berkeley study.) The point is that when proposals for curricular changes designed to accommodate the nature of students are made, it is well to remember that most of the information about the nature of students comes from a "'pooling of impressions' [and] the pool is less inclusive and the impressions less reliable than they might be" (Sw., p. 261).

A second observation concerns student disenchantment with general education programs. Most of these studies, except those at Brown and Stanford, were completed before the student complaints about "relevance" became as strident as they have lately been, and the discussions in most of the reports make little direct reference to this issue. However, the issue is clearly there—as a principal factor in the decision to undertake the study, if nothing else. The proposals made represent attempts to deal with this question of student disenchantment in terms of the content of curricula—and quite properly so. However, much of the disenchantment is also a function of the problems of teaching and advising discussed in preceding chapters. In many institutions, the general education and introductory courses (which serve to meet distribution requirements) are the courses which are taught in large, impersonal classes and frequently rely heavily on graduate students as instructors. Furthermore, while there are many notable exceptions, a great many faculty members find general education courses remote from the specialized areas of research and advanced teaching which most interest them. For this reason appropriate time and effort may not always go into the preparation and conduct of these courses. As the Stanford committee observed in the passage quoted earlier, the faculty member "prefers to teach what *he* wants to teach and learn, not what is prescribed by a committee."[8]

A third observation concerns the fact that restrictions of almost any kind—but especially traditional ones—are not particularly fashionable today among students. "In a day when 'legitimacy' is a watchword, the university should be very sure indeed that its rules have a defensible rationale, an impossible task in the context of the General Studies Program" (Stan., p. 9). Whether the task is in fact impossible is a matter about which judgments will vary, but few would dispute that any requirements must be supported by a most thorough and sound rationale if they are to have legitimacy in this "permissive" era.

The study committees, then, have intended to relate general education programs to the apparent nature and background of today's students. Perhaps the committees have achieved this, but unhappily it is quite likely that neither they nor the institutions they represent know a great deal about those students. It is quite certain that they know far less than modern research and data storage and retrieval techniques would permit.

**CONCLUSION**  Ultimately, the problems of designing general education programs seem to be less a function of the preparation and the value systems of students than of the issue discussed earlier in this chapter: the very great difficulties faced by faculty members in collectively designing and implementing such programs. One difficulty is posed by the almost overwhelming amount of knowledge and the multitude of techniques for dealing with knowledge which must be somehow encompassed. A second difficulty is the zeal with which most faculty members guard their individualism and their professionalism. This zeal, combined with the increasing size and complexity of the universities and of most colleges, makes the traditional, collegial process of decision making a near-shambles.

Beyond these social and institutional constraints—powerful as they are—one senses a possible loss of confidence. The Harvard *Redbook,* which has influenced so much of our thinking about

---

[8] At present, many students and perhaps some faculty members would add to this sentence, "or what the *students* want to learn."

general education, is called "General Education in a Free Society." When it was written in 1945, most Americans showed an optimistic confidence that American society was, and would continue to be, free and viable. From this confidence flowed a broad consensus about the qualities of, and the qualifications for, citizenship and a meaningful life in that society. Men could and did have a zest for working out the educational basis for citizenship and living in that society. When, as seems so often to be the case today, confidence and consensus are replaced by doubt, uncertainty, and even anguish, such zest is rather hard to come by.

# 15. *Curriculum: The Major and Other Matters*

As the preceding chapter indicated, structured general education programs have virtually no support, and distribution requirements retain only reluctant support. On the other hand, what may be called "nonspecialization" remains a powerful force. All the studies proposed various arrangements designed to ensure that undergraduate education would consist of more than just professional and specialized learning. "Educational lopsidedness," as the Stanford report put it, should be avoided. On the other hand, a commitment to some "knowledge in depth," the idea behind the traditional major, is still strong.

What the several reports had to say about the major is discussed in the following section. Following that are reviews of the studies' proposals regarding the nature of introductory courses, upper-level courses, independent study, and freshman seminars. Finally, the chapter covers the reports' proposals concerning grading and overall course loads. These latter are only marginally related to curriculum, but the reasoning behind them is generally rather closely related to that which supports the maintenance of nonspecialization, and so they are included here.

THE MAJOR All the institutions studied required a major or concentration, yet only a few of the studies had much to say about its form and content. This appears to be forbidden territory for college or university committees, the vigilantly guarded turf of the departments. As Daniel Bell said, "It is difficult, of course, for 'outsiders' to challenge a department's decision about what is relevant or necessary to a field" (1966, p. 256).

If such challenges are difficult for faculty outsiders to make, it will certainly be difficult for students to make them. While none of the reports suggested so directly, it seems likely that the inability of students (or faculties generally) to influence the content of the typical departmental major explains why nearly all the studies recommended that students be permitted to design their own majors. (A fairly vigorous review of the student's plan would be required.) At some institutions—Duke and Wesleyan, for example—this would be done within the departmental framework. In others, such as Stanford, UCLA, and Brown, some more broadly based body would provide a "home" for these students. On the whole, the committees appear to expect only a relatively few, highly motivated students to take this option. Presumably to accommodate students who are not interested in the regular departmental majors but who lack the motivation to design their own, several reports proposed the introduction or expansion of interdepartmental majors. Daniel Bell attacked the same problem in a somewhat different way by proposing that each department design a "second-track" major "for those who want, not detailed preparation in a discipline for graduate work, but a broad background" (1966, p. 293). One other limitation was proposed by the New Hampshire and Stanford committees; they recommended that the major department not be allowed to specify more than one-half of all the courses taken by the student.[1]

With the exception of Bell's proposal for second tracks, these recommendations would have relatively little effect on the programs of the mass of students, who would presumably continue to take a regular departmental major. Most of the studies more or less left it at that. Only the Michigan State and Brown reports delved more deeply into the nature and content of the major.

The Michigan State committee made a very forthright attack on a problem which must be very nearly unique to that institution: 170 major fields available to undergraduate students. However, the committee's observations have a considerable degree of relevance even to institutions with far fewer major fields:

A university must choose with greatest care what it will teach. It must, to remain a university, teach *all* of the basic disciplines and *none* of the applied fields which are altogether removed from them. But this leaves a wide range of choices still to be made, choices which must result from the most judicious assessment of social needs and values as well as more

---

[1] New Hampshire would permit a tightly controlled exemption for formally accredited programs. Stanford would require the accredited engineering departments to offer a nonaccredited program which would meet this limitation.

mundane, but vital, considerations of available human and physical resources. . . .

The committee . . . has become convinced that certain fields now offered do not, by their total lack of connection with or dependence upon basic disciplines, warrant a place in the University, and that still others do not speak to social needs of high priority . . . (MS, pp. 74–75).

The committee followed this by proposing that there be instituted, at the university level, "a regular review process designed to insure that all curricula in the University can continue to be justified in terms of broad social needs and University resources" (MS, p. 76). The committee also proposed that all majors surviving this review be subjected to another review at the departmental and college level to ensure that they would have a "degree of coherence and sequential pattern" and that they would neither be too loosely prescribed nor offer too little student choice.

The Michigan State report did not identify majors which failed to meet the criteria set forth, but lest anyone assume that the concerns which the Michigan State committee expressed are those of only large public universities, which are likely to have some rather narrowly vocational programs, the following excerpts from the Brown report are included to indicate that excessive professionalism is, rather, a universal situation:

Concentration may coincide in some ways with specific prerequisite training for a student's professional goals, but pre-professional training is not a central aspect of the concentration process. Liberal, as opposed to specifically pre-professional, concentration is designed to carry out the process of intellectual and personal development which are at the center of the undergraduate educational experience.

The values of the concentration for the personal and intellectual development of the student should be its central purpose. Although this may slightly hinder the speed with which the future academician may acquire the necessary skills of the discipline, it will in the long run aid the development of true professionals (Br., pp. 19–22).

The Brown committee proposed that each student design his own major, although ". . . department and interdepartmental groups of faculty may establish, subject to approval and periodic review . . . standard programs of concentration." Students could, and no doubt many would, elect these standard programs. However, if the approval and review process does in fact ensure that the programs will be liberal rather than specifically preprofessional, more students may have a different experience. That this may not be easy to do is suggested by the observation of the Toronto committee that the

> . . . supposed demands of graduate work [and the] knowledge explosion [have] led to the attitude, within the Faculty, that no student is to be taken seriously if he is not aiming at a career in the specialty, and, among the students, that no learning or insight is to be taken seriously unless it is clearly going to be professionally useful (Tor., p. 57).

In sum, then, the major or concentration remains a focal point in undergraduate education. Since few of these reports really discuss the matter, there was apparently never any question but that it should so remain. A few reports did delve into the basic nature of the major, but none included any serious analysis of what an undergraduate program might be without a major. One may assume that we are here in the realm of revealed truth.

On the other hand, most of the studies recommended provision for majors outside the control of the academic departments. If significant numbers of students were to pick up the option which most of these reports would give them, to design their own majors, some important changes might result. Until very recently, one would have predicted, along with the Toronto committee, that students with an eye on graduate school or a job would make little use of the option. It is less easy, today, to be confident about predicting student behavior and values.

INTRODUC-
TORY
COURSES
Nearly all the studies reflected the view of the Stanford committee "that greater attention needs to be paid to providing courses that are not merely introductory to further work but that can serve as an intelligent layman's introduction to the subject matter" (Stan., p. 26). The Berkeley committee called for introductory courses with "increased flexibility wherever these courses need not be vigorously sequential" (Berk., p. 126), but several others echoed the proposal made by the UCLA committee:

> The two major functions of an introductory course are *either* to introduce majors to the field of specialization *or* to make the field comprehensible to the general student. The second function should not be sacrificed to the first. If the demands of the first are so confining as to deny the realization of the second, special sections or courses should be established . . . (UCLA, p. 25).

None of the studies really attempted to spell out what such courses would be like, and the New Hampshire committee, while recommending "multiple-track" introductory courses, recognized "that this approach carried with it the danger that the nonmajor courses will become second-rate" (N.H., p. 64). One problem with these courses, and with all "nondiscipline" courses, is that they may lack real substance and vigor because the faculty member is likely to be on increasingly thin intellectual ice as he moves away from his area of competence. The second problem concerns the academic system of promotion and compensation. If these depend largely on one's standing in one's professional specialty, one is reluctant to get shunted aside in developing "general education" courses. On every campus one hears, "I would love to develop a new course for nonmajors, but I'll lose out in my department if I do."[2] One solution to these problems may be to have jointly taught courses. This would tend to ensure that these courses would not lack substance, and it would not require the faculty member to "spread himself too thin." Another solution may be simply to offer the courses, and if enough students voluntarily take them, perhaps there will be sufficient pressure to ensure that they do not become second rate.

**UPPER-LEVEL COURSES**    Apart from Daniel Bell's third-tier courses, which would be a part of the structured general education program,[3] several of the reports proposed increased development of nonspecialized courses to be offered as electives at the upper level. The Michigan State committee noted that students "are either encouraged to take or freely elect to take liberal education courses outside their major beyond those required by the general education program," but observed that there must be an "extension in the number and variety of appropriate 'non-major' courses in the liberal arts and sciences" (MS, p. 67) if the requirement or election is to be meaningful.

Brown had had a number of "university courses" since the late 1950s, and expansion of such offerings was recommended there. These courses "are intended to provide opportunities at a relatively advanced level of analytical competence for the student to achieve a wider perspective than may ordinarily be available in depart-

---

[2] It is also true, of course, that many who have not made it in their specialty or have become bored with it suddenly develop an interest in general education.

[3] See pp. 171–172.

mental offerings" (Br., p. 25). These courses might be inter-disciplinary and problem- or theme-centered, relating a discipline to a broader historical context. The committee presumed that most students would take one or more of these courses. The Berkeley committee referred to the Brown courses as a model for the sort of thing it recommended (Berk., p. 131), and the Stanford report referred to "science and technology for the non-specialist" as typical of a suitable area for development of new courses. The Stanford committee also recommended that the professional schools offer courses for "outside" students.[4] The Michigan State committee was concerned not only with courses at the advanced level for nonmajors but also with courses which would "reinforce the [major] student's understanding of the relationship of his particular major field to others allied with it at a level of sophistication appropriate to the final year of undergraduate study" (MS, p. 68). The committee urged that these be college, not departmental, courses.

**INDEPENDENT AND FIELD STUDY**  All the institutions considered here had some form of independent study, and most of the reports urged that it be expanded and made more readily available. It was stated or implied in several of the reports that relatively little use is made of independent study, and the following, taken from the Michigan State report, possibly suggests why:

> The main weakness of our present commitment to independent study is its occasional aimlessness. A student may have a vague notion that he would like to learn much more about Freud's thought but he does not know to whom to turn for guidance in organizing further reading and he does not know which professors would be willing to supervise and evaluate his efforts. And so he must search until he finds (if he does) an already over-committed member of the faculty who in spite of other obligations agrees to supervise the study. A program so organized (and arranged on an over-load basis for the instructor) is not likely to succeed as often as it should (MS, pp. 81–82).

---

[4] As one who has generally been a member of a professional school, I very much agree with the Stanford committee's observation that the "intellectual resources [in these schools] can mean a great deal to undergraduates, especially because they represent career patterns and life styles that will eventually absorb a significant proportion of the undergraduate population" (Stan., II, p. 26). Business, engineering, and law schools, for example, could and should offer relevant and liberal courses for the nonprofessional student.

The Stanford committee reviewed some of the same problems. Like the Michigan State committee, it proposed better organization and more money as remedies. While the enthusiasm for independent study is fairly widespread, the indications are that when it is grafted on to a system of regular courses, lectures, and the like— especially in an institution with many students—it simply does not work very well. Widespread independent study would involve a near-revolution in the organization and processes of most institutions, and none of the studies really considered this.

A number of the institutions already had programs for study abroad (Stanford's is undoubtedly the most elaborate in the country). Continuation of these was recommended, and in some cases—Berkeley, Swarthmore, and Wesleyan particularly—expansion of "field study" was urged: "We feel that a sustained piece of outside work which the student is qualified to undertake and which can be evaluated by the faculty for its intellectual context is a proper object of academic recognition" (Berk., p. 138). At Swarthmore it was proposed to grant up to one semester's credit for practical work done off campus, "when it can be shown to lend itself to intellectual analysis and is likely to contribute to a student's progress in regular course work . . ." (Sw., p. 66).

At Wesleyan, granting a semester off for the purpose of doing off-campus work was proposed, although initially at any rate, such work was not to carry academic credit. The goals for this program are worth pondering for what they imply about "on-campus" education:

First, to focus on different material. Second, to enhance motivation, assuming that such motivation will carry over into on-campus learning. Third, to generate concerns and ideas in the student that may help him decide on what course, major fields, distinction topic, perhaps even life work, he is really after. Fourth, to shake up faculty and curriculum (Wes., V, p. 6).

**FRESHMAN SEMINARS** Several of the studies recommended a program of freshman seminars. The Berkeley proposal is typical:

Such freshman seminars should consist of groups of no more than twelve students, taught by members of the faculty in whatever areas of intellectual discourse a faculty member is inclined to meet with entering students. The subject matter of all such seminars need not be strictly determined as long as the orientation is one of dialogue and the spirit of inquiry. Each faculty member offering a freshman seminar would act as academic advisor to the seminar students (Berk., p. 138).

These seminars are designed only in part as a way of ensuring a degree of nonspecialization. They are also intended, as the last sentence quoted above implies, to meet some of the problems of orientation and advising encountered by most students. Characteristic of most of them were:

... that they be outlets or avenues for development of personal interests (not strictly professional interests, necessarily) of faculty members; second, that they get students and faculty working together in an intensive and advanced investigation; and third, that they be distinct additions to the curriculum, not simply imitating existing courses but affording a special experience (Sw., p. 96).

At institutions where such seminars were not proposed—Brown and Duke—other arrangements were in effect or proposed. At Brown, the modes-of-thought courses would have limited enrollments and would be essentially nonspecialized in content. The Duke study did not propose freshman seminars as that term is used here, but did recommend that each student—in each of his first two years—have the equivalent of two semester courses taught in one of several small group formats.

The great difficulty with such programs, of course, is that they are uncommonly expensive when simply grafted onto existing programs. In most universities most students do have a few small classes—almost always in advanced courses taken in the junior and senior years. Most universities simply cannot afford—and could not provide the necessary faculty even if money were not an issue—to have nothing but small classes. Consequently, a freshman seminar program really calls for a reallocation of resources within the institution. Such a reallocation will come only after a widespread acceptance of the proposition that general and relatively personal instruction for freshmen is more important than specialized and personal instruction for upperclassmen. While most of the reports recommend freshman seminars, none really comes to grips with this issue.

GRADING   The idea of grading student performance in courses has never been wholly approved or accepted, but grading has been a feature of higher education in this country (and every other country) for a very long time. In recent years, something of an assault—especially by students—has been mounted against grades, and some, though not all, of the studies joined in that assault.

The Berkeley study proposed what has become a fairly standard approach: In each term, a student could take one course on a pass–not pass basis. Courses required for the student's major would be excluded from this unless the major department agreed to permit it. The Berkeley committee also proposed that grades earned by a student during his first term in the university not be included in his grade-point average.[5] This latter proposal rather anticipates the Swarthmore recommendation that only pass or fail grades be recorded on the student's transcript for the freshman year.

At Stanford, it was recommended that only A, B, and C be retained in the grading scale, with D and F being eliminated. A failed course would not be recorded on the student's record, the only penalty being loss of credit. Any course—if the instructor wished it and his department approved—could be graded on a pass basis in lieu of letter grades, and the student could take any number of such courses. Brown would give the instructor the same option, but would permit the student to elect to have all his courses graded on a pass basis. As at Stanford, failed courses would not appear on the student's record. (This system is apparently coming to be known as "pass-erase" at Stanford.)

**Reasons for Changes** All the colleges and universities included here (except Toronto) employed the more or less standard American system of using grades A to F and combining them into a grade-point average variously referred to as "GPA," "accume," "cume," or "point." In assessing this system and its impact on the education of students, the committees displayed, more than anything else, uncertainty about its validity and ambivalence about changes to be made. The essential problem, as the Muscatine Committee put it, is that ". . . as more and more students compete for admission to our better undergraduate and graduate schools, they have become increasingly 'grade conscious.' Students, faculty, and administrators alike have expressed concern about the pressure of grades . . ." (Berk., p. 93).

There was agreement that grading creates fear and anxiety,

[5] This proposal was voted down by the Academic Senate.

neither of which is conducive to real learning. Further, the system is "deceptively refined" (Stan., II, p. 46) and "inadequate in the dimensions of work that it measures and the amount of information about progress that it provides" (Sw., p. 98).

In spite of these declared weaknesses of a grading system, all the studies accepted the necessity for some evaluation of student performance, and while Swarthmore and Brown considered the possibility of relying on written comments for evaluation of student performance, the basic idea of some grading system was not really challenged. The Swarthmore study suggested that conventional grades were, in effect, a convenient summation of written comments, the latter being almost impossible to handle administratively. Brown pointed to another widely recognized problem: the graduate schools. Several of the institutions reported on here send large numbers of their graduates on to graduate school, and the others have significant numbers who do further academic work. As the Brown report pointed out, ". . . the risks involved to the student who wants to enter graduate or professional school might be considerable if all grades were to be eliminated entirely at this time" (Br., p. 33).

Thus, while several of the studies proposed moves designed to take the sting out of grading—proposals which ranged from permitting the student to elect a few pass-fail courses outside his major field to the total pass-erase system of Brown and Stanford—none really rejected the idea of evaluation. The reports did not challenge fully the contention of Jencks and Riesman that the basic function of the American college may be "certification."

**ACADEMIC WORK LOADS**  The discussions about grading involved some recognition that in the "better" schools, at any rate, a competitive, hardworking atmosphere had become the norm. This same recognition was reflected in the several suggestions for reducing the number of courses taken by students. Many of the institutions which operated on the semester system and which required five or more courses generally proposed a reduction to four. Stanford proposed a shift from a four-course quarter to a four-course semester. UCLA suggested the possibility of reducing from four to three the number of courses taken in a quarter.

In general the committees argued that existing course loads were too heavy to permit a leisurely yet penetrating exploration of a subject. "We feel that students now are sometimes overburdened with academic busy work," wrote the Duke committee (Duke, p. 13). The Swarthmore report suggested "that the workload contributes to a pervasive sense of dissatisfaction about assignments that have been slighted and of guilt about the cost of extra-curricular pursuits to course work. . . ." (Sw., p. 90).

Most of the studies, however, were more concerned about fragmentation of the student's time and attention than about the amount of work:

> Whatever the relative number of hours involved it seems clear that there is a limit to the number of different subjects with which a student can come to grips at any particular time. There can be little more than a superficial exposure involved when a student is simultaneously considering six, seven, even eight different subjects. Mastery in some depth, which is one objective of the educational process, is clearly impossible under such circumstances (NH, p. 56).

On the whole, the reports suggest that the day of the "gentieman's C" has passed, and while none recommend a return to that more casual era, they did convey a sense that some redressing of the balance is called for.

**CONCLUSION**  Beyond the matters of course load and grading, this chapter has described a number of approaches to the maintenance and expansion of opportunities for students to engage in nonspecialized study beyond the regular, formal, general education programs. While most reports did not give much consideration to the contents of the departmental majors, several did propose student-designed majors as substitutes. All these proposals in some degree challenge the interests and the objectives of the specialized departments. They involve at least some elimination of the hegemony of the departments over the curriculum. Collectively, these proposals would require modification in the value system of the academic revolution that gives primacy to professional, discipline-oriented study. Most of the committees recognized this implication of what they were proposing and recommended administrative arrangements designed to support these curricular changes.

# 16. Organization and Administration

"It seems high time for some university to challenge the conception that the department is the sole context within which scholarship can flourish" (Wes., VII, p. 5).

These bold words appeared in one of the working papers of the Wesleyan study, and while none of the committees—including Wesleyan's—made such a challenge directly, virtually all of them recognized the issue and attempted to mount an indirect challenge. The nature of these challenges and the reasoning behind them are the subject of this short chapter, which, in spite of its brevity, may be more important than all that has gone before. Most of the institutions encountered very great difficulty in coming to grips with the challenges to the *status quo* proposed by these reports, and those who prepared the reports anticipated this condition and tried to do something about it in advance.

The problem boils down to the following:

At the present moment specialization is more likely to be protected and nurtured than is education in breadth. The basic instructional, research and administrative unit is the department, and the department is clearly tied to the discipline—to specialization. The growth of graduate level instruction reinforces the influence of the discipline-oriented departments, since it is almost exclusively concerned with specialization. The organization of the departments into colleges at the undergraduate level does little to diminish the central influence of the departments or disciplines in the determination of educational policy. Indeed, given the *Realpolitik* of college governance, the structure probably reinforces the influence of the specialized departments. The allocation of funds within the University is primarily related to the disciplines (NH, p. 17).

The Wesleyan study carried an analysis of the effects of this a little further: "Intellectual community is sliced into separate

pieces and disintegrates [and] a scholar who wishes to pursue subjects or follow procedures that do not fit within a given department
gets looked down upon and may experience homelessness" (Wes.,
VII, p. 5). A dramatic quotation on this theme could be taken from
nearly all the reports, but let Daniel Bell have the last, rather
succinct word: ". . . departments in the university exist in inglorious
isolation from each other, intellectually as well as organizationally"
(1966, p. 67).

None of this is new, of course. Robert Hutchins is only the best
known (and perhaps the best phrasemaker) of those who have commented on the issue in this generation and previous ones. A renewed attack is made in these studies because they were in varying
degrees trying to wrest control of at least some of the education of
undergraduates from the discipline-oriented departments—the
"scholarly guilds," in what is, I believe, David Riesman's phrase.
They reflect an awareness that without some countervailing force
beyond either ideology or logic, the hegemony of the departments
would not be disturbed and therefore educational policy would not
be much changed.

Most of the reports proposed the creation of new administrative
posts whose *raisons d'être* would be to "exercise a continuing review of . . . education of undergraduates, to support and maintain
what is good, to aid in the renovation of what is inadequate, and to
stimulate and assist educational innovation" (Stan., X, p. 45). The
titles varied—dean of undergraduate studies (Stanford), dean for
general education (New Hampshire), and vice-provost for undergraduate education (Michigan State), for example—but the job
descriptions were much the same everywhere. In the short run, the
purpose was to provide top-level direction for the implementation
of other recommendations of the report, and in the longer run to be
a continuing center for initiation and support of experimentation,
innovation, and change.[1]

In making these proposals, all the committees displayed a decent
respect for the opinion of faculty members (quite generally held)
that a "proliferation of administrators" is always deplorable. Most
approached their recommendation somewhat .apologetically: "We

---

[1] Brown did not propose a new administrative position, but the committee
on modes-of-thought courses would have somewhat the same role. UCLA had
a recently appointed vice-chancellor for educational planning and programs,
but a council for educational development was proposed as well. Among the
reports reviewed here, only Duke's included no mention of this problem.

are reluctant to recommend any addition to the formal academic administrative apparatus," confessed the Toronto committee (Tor., p. 79), but the need to meet the effects of "inglorious isolation" overcame the reluctance.

Many of the reports considered the problems of status and power involved in adding a new level to the administrative hierarchy. Each of the institutions had at least one academic dean; in most places they were legion. All but Swarthmore had a provost or vice-chancellor or vice-president who was concerned essentially with academic matters.[2] The evidence in the reports—entirely negative, of course—is that these officials were largely the prisoners of departmental power, for otherwise there would have been no need for the new administrators. The problem is that short of a coup d'état, the very departments and colleges whose power and influence the committees desired to have controlled would have to accept the idea of the new post. Pretty clearly, they would not agree to any real transfer of power or status. To establish such a post under these conditions would strain the talents and imagination of the very best management specialist, and, on the whole, the committees ducked the hard organizational constraints and relied on goodwill and faith:

It is easy to overstate the importance of administrative arrangements. . . . The talents called for [are] tact, educational sensitivity, and ability to minimize resistance to change (Stan., p. 45).

. . . his relationships with college deans and with departments will have to be worked out, but we believe that the benefit to all . . . will give the necessary impetus to working out these relationships (NH, p. 26).

The incumbent . . . should not have a position of line authority with respect to the deans of colleges, but . . . his influence and specific range of duties should not be a matter of doubt (MS, p. 116).

Ultimately, the exercise of power tends to be rather closely related to the possession of money. "Budgetary leverage," as the Stanford study rather delicately called it, is essential to changing anything of consequence. The Michigan State study proposed such budgetary leverage for its vice-provost, observing that "Without

---

[2] The Swarthmore report proposed appointment of a provost in part to deal with the problem being discussed here.

budget decision-making powers, the administrator is indeed a paper tiger . . ." (MS, p. 118). No one would dispute these contentions, but unfortunately they scarcely solve the problem with which the committees were dealing. It has been a very long time since any college or university has had enough money, and during the period when most of these reports were completed, the institutions involved were generally entering a period when the annual availability of "new money" was being sharply curtailed. Thus to give someone control of scarce funds for a new activity will require taking them away from someone else. The reports were silent on the implications of this, and given the fact that the departments and colleges in most universities have an important voice in the basic decisions about allocation of funds, one may be less than sanguine about the likelihood of any real budgetary leverage for the new administrator. Stanford's experience should prove enlightening, for the yet-to-be selected dean of undergraduate studies has been given, in principle, both a budget and a voice in faculty hiring and retention.

If one agrees with the Brown report that the "intellectual and personal development (self-realization) of the student" is the primary purpose of undergraduate education, he may see these proposals as speaking to the most fundamental issue raised in these reports: some redressing of the balance between that purpose on the one hand and professional interests which tend to have other conflicting purposes on the other hand. The imbalance is apparent in any of the problems—teaching, curriculum, and the rest—with which these reports have been concerned. On the whole, the studies have attempted to meet this need by creating new power centers without—overtly, at any rate—disturbing the old, to make an omelet without breaking any eggs. "Tact, educational sensitivity, and the ability to minimize resistance to change" are highly desirable qualities in an administrator, but if power within the university is to be shifted and if, through this shift the directions of the university are to be changed, some eggs will surely have to be broken.

# 17. The Processes of Change

Each of the situations reviewed here involves an attempt to change the basic educational policies of a college or university. While the scope and degree of the proposed changes vary, all have in common the use of the traditional, collegial process of study, analysis, discussion, and debate leading to a decision based on general acceptability. What follows is a comparison of the cases in terms of particular elements in this overall process: institutional climate, committee makeup and procedures, degree of involvement, reports, leadership, and institutional size and character. Such an analysis of the elements in a complex process involves a risk of oversimplification, since it is obviously not possible to separate these elements completely. The Swarthmore case, for example, illustrates effective leadership, but Swarthmore is a small, homogeneous college and as such is probably more susceptible to leadership than a large, heterogeneous university. On the other hand, Dean Allen of Toronto demonstrated effective leadership in a large, heterogeneous institution, but he was greatly assisted by the effective employment of "student power." In other words, while the elements of the process may and will be isolated for purposes of discussion, their interrelatedness at a particular place and time must always be recognized.[1]

**THE INSTITUTIONAL CLIMATE** Unhappily, the results of these studies seem to lend support—at least in a negative way—to the efficacy of pressure politics as a way of bringing about change. There is little indication in any of the experiences to support the idea that the study-and-report technique is an effective way of gaining acceptance of the *need* for change or

---

[1] The reader should be reminded here of the earlier discussion of the limitations on judgments made about the success of any of the studies. (See pp. 7–8.)

of creating enthusiasm for involvement in developing new policies. Where the study-and-report processes were intended primarily to challenge the *status quo,* they largely failed to do so. When the essential objective was to develop the details of a change in the *status quo* after the community[2] had already accepted the need for some change, the study-and-report processes were much more effective.

At Duke and at Swarthmore, most of the recommendations of the committees were accepted, and accepted in a relatively short period of time—short, at least, as time for decision making is measured in academia. In both cases, there was relatively widespread acceptance of the idea that changes were needed before the studies began. That the curriculum needed to be substantially less restrictive was generally agreed upon at Duke before the study began.[3] The need for making some changes in the processes of honors and for providing faculty members with more time and support for research was accepted by a great many at Swarthmore before the Commission on Educational Policy was formed. Indeed, this acceptance was an important element in the decision to form the commission. This is not to deny that both of these studies moved beyond the original issues and made recommendations which were quite contentious. Both did. Nevertheless, neither of these studies had to prepare the ground for their specific proposals by first convincing large numbers in the community that certain changes were necessary. The Wesleyan study, too, resulted in changes for which the ground had already been prepared—coeducation, for example—but it did not succeed in bringing about a fundamental reexamination of the basic nature of the university, which had been the intent of the president and the provost.

Columbia, Michigan State, and New Hampshire all began their studies because a senior administrator wanted to create an atmos-

[2] Many of the institutions included in this study are moving toward a significantly broadened role for students in decision-making processes, but in the situations described here, formal decision-making power rested mostly with the faculty or—for some specific issues—with the administration. Thus community here means the faculty and, sometimes, faculty and administration.

[3] It may well be true that the general acceptance of the Duke report is also related to the fact that it made only 11 proposals, most of which were rather closely related. The implications of acceptance were probably much more readily discernible to the faculty as a whole than was the case in most other institutions where larger numbers of recommendations about a wide-ranging number of topics were made.

phere for the acceptance of change and then to bring about actual changes. In all three cases, the extent of changes made as a result of the studies was rather limited. The study groups themselves certainly became convinced of the need for fundamental changes, but their reports failed to arouse a similar conviction among large numbers of their colleagues, even though the two committee reports and Bell's book were most forthright in their extensive analyses of why changes were needed.

**External Pressure** The Brown and Toronto situations seem to contradict the generalization that prior acceptance of the need for change is essential for success. Both of these studies led to some rather far-ranging changes, and yet neither was launched in an atmosphere of readiness for change. The origins of the Toronto study were essentially the same as those of the Columbia, New Hampshire, and Michigan State studies. The Brown study was initiated by a student rather than an administrator but for the same reason: to create an atmosphere for change. Neither of the studies created much of a stir among the faculties involved when it first appeared. Both, however, captured the interest of students and to a considerable extent were carried through because of student pressure. One can only guess what would have happened without that pressure, but the facts of each case support the hypothesis that little real change would have resulted.[4]

The Berkeley study, in a way, illustrates both points. There was a certain degree of preexisting acceptance of the need for change at Berkeley which was instrumental in the decision to undertake the study. On the other hand, that acceptance was largely a response to external pressure created by the Free Speech Movement. As the impact of that affair receded over time, so did the acceptance of the need for change.

One must be somewhat more tentative about the uncompleted Stanford study, but to date it appears to conform to the pattern being described. It was started by a president who wished to bring about change, but at least in some degree it was also a response to student pressure, which was in evidence throughout. Many of its achievements to date—changes in admissions and residential policies, for example—concern matters where the need for some

[4] One must also recognize that acceptance under pressure may be more nominal than real. At Toronto, I feel that the acceptance will prove to have been real. It is too soon to tell about Brown.

changes was generally accepted before the study began. It is not certain that student support was responsible for acceptance of the dean for undergraduate studies, but it surely helped. And those areas—teaching and curriculum—in which proposals still have to be made or accepted are those in which there does not appear to have been general acceptance of the need for change.

**Summary**  The situations reviewed here suggest that these studies have rarely succeeded in bringing about any fundamental change in educational policies on the campuses involved except where a significant portion of the faculty had accepted the desirability of some change before the study began or where pressures for change from outside the faculties were much in evidence.

**THE COMMITTEES**  With the possible exception of the Los Angeles committee, all appear to have become effective and dedicated working groups. Faculty members are criticized (even by some of these study committees) for their growing involvement with matters such as research and consulting which remove them from active participation in the educational affairs of their university, but each of these committees is testimony to the willingness of some of them to devote untold hours to educational matters—often with frustration as the principal reward.

In general, these committees are also testimony to the ability of men[5] when given a task of consequence to learn to work together to complete the task. None of these groups had worked together before, and many members were not known to one another before the first meeting; yet with the exception of the Berkeley committee, all seem to have been able to resolve their differences over issues. In no committee did opposing camps develop (again excepting Berkeley), and while each report contained one or two carefully worked-out compromises, they all seem to have achieved a widespread and genuine consensus. It is true that some of the studies challenged the status and the norms of the particular institution less than others, and so consensus may have been easier to achieve in some cases. The Los Angeles committee appears to have achieved only a min-

[5] It is at least worth noting that with the exception of one of the outside members of the Swarthmore committee and the dean of Pembroke *ex-officio* on the Brown committee, no women were involved in these studies. Some few important faculty posts have recently gone to women, but male dominance of educational policy making appears to be unshaken.

imum sort of consensus. Nevertheless, each of these groups was able to work its way through to a somewhat changed view of the institution of which the members were a part.

With perhaps two exceptions, the cases do not suggest that this ability to work together was a criterion for committee membership. The care with which members were chosen varied considerably. At Swarthmore and Toronto an attempt was made to choose people who would probably be compatible. Elsewhere, this factor was left mostly to chance. In the larger universities, there was some effort to represent the important subdivisions or areas of the curriculum, but there was much less effort to build a committee which would be a balanced sample of diverse faculty views about the content and processes of education. On the contrary, there was some bias toward persons known to be concerned with education in general and with the particular university. However, given that only Swarthmore is the kind of institution in which "everybody knows everybody else" there was, fundamentally, a considerable degree of chance in the selection of these committees. In spite of this, or because of it, they did become effective working groups.

With the possible exception of the Los Angeles committee, each group seems to have completed its task to general applause, even from those who would not accept its recommendations. There was certainly no case where the membership of the committee was a consequential influence on the nature of ultimate faculty response to its proposals—no case, that is, where proposals were rejected because of who made them.

It may well be that the effective functioning of these committees is raw material for studying group dynamics (not a part of this project), but it does not appear to have much bearing on educational policy formulation. The fact that nearly all the committees worked effectively as committees did not particularly increase their impact on the institutions of which they were a part. Effective committees appear to have been unable to overcome the absence of a widespread acceptance of the need for change, nor were they able to overcome a lack of effective leadership in the process of consideration and implementation. Furthermore, the lack of impact of Daniel Bell's report at Columbia does not suggest that having one person prepare the basic document intended to lead to change will be any more effective than having a committee do so. Who prepares one of these studies does not appear to be a generally significant variable in the overall outcome. On the other hand, most members of most of the committees with whom I talked spoke warmly of the value of the work to them. All felt that they had learned much from the long discussions and had come out of the work with a much greater understanding of the problems and the potential of their university. Many spoke of the degree to which the intensive work together had permitted them to get well beyond the barriers usually existing between the disciplines, and they mentioned changes in many aspects of their work which resulted. All this, of course, may be merely sentimental, but barriers to effective communication and broadly based action exist in most universities, and no opportunity to break through them should be missed. At this level, the fact that most of these committees became very effective working groups is an important consequence of the studies.

**INVOLVEMENT**  In one way or another, all the study committees tried to involve other members of the university in their work. No group went to the mountain top to deliberate and to return with its proposals full-blown. (This is not to deny that many committee members did become rather messianic about educational reform as a result of their work.) All seemed to feel from the start that they needed interest and involvement from those who would have to accept and implement the proposals. One committee member said, "We hoped to have general agreement on most of our recommendations before they were formally made."

The most common approaches to securing involvement were to hold open hearings, to request written and oral submissions,[6] and to meet with departments and similar groups. The New Hampshire committee went well beyond these devices by issuing a preliminary report and organizing campus-wide study groups to consider it. The extreme approach to involvement was taken at Wesleyan, where there was no committee as such but where, at one time or another, virtually every member of the faculty was "on the study." Stanford also followed this approach by having a steering committee of faculty members and students coordinating and summarizing the work of innumerable topic committees. These latter involved large numbers of faculty members and students during the course of the study.

There is little to suggest that openness on the part of the study

---

[6] The rate of response to these requests, it will be recalled, was generally quite low.

committee and involvement of other members of the university in developing recommendations have much independent effect on the outcome of the study. One would guess that two factors are at work here: the propensity of most individuals not to face up to issues until they absolutely have to and the fact that most people are wary of making an early commitment to any possible change which will affect them and their work. The necessity for busy people to pass by anything which does not directly affect them is probably also involved. After the Macpherson report at Toronto had been public for nearly a year, Dean Allen announced in a faculty meeting that a committee was to draw up and present to the faculty in two weeks' time legislation to implement certain of the Macpherson proposals. A number of faculty members took the floor to complain of the short time allowed to consider "such momentous changes." Dean Allen responded that it was his experience that no matter how much time was allowed, most faculty members did not study proposals until just before the meeting called to consider them. At several of the universities, informal polls were taken—usually by the student newspaper sometime after the report had been issued—to see how much attention it had received. The results of these were much the same: A minority of the faculty had actually read the report, and another minority did not even know it existed. (All faculty members were sent copies in all cases.)

One cannot say that a series of proposals prepared *in camera* and abruptly presented for action would have been more or less successful because none was handled in this way. One can say that the several attempts made to involve people—to get them to "participate," as current fashion has it—did not seem to expand greatly the likelihood of bringing about change.

THE REPORTS The principal problems of educational policy that the several reports discussed and the solutions to these problems which they proposed were discussed earlier. Quite apart from specific policy recommendations, however, the overall character of these reports does appear to have been a factor of some consequence in the ultimate outcome of the studies.

Each of these reports—in one way or another and in varying degrees—is based upon some rather fundamental views about higher education and about the particular institution. Only the Los Angeles and Toronto reports failed to make some statement of general principles about education in the particular institution, and even those two reports recommended that such a statement be developed by another committee. The extensiveness and the explicitness of such statements vary, but the reader can extract from the reports the basic foundations of the committees' general posture.[7] Most of the recommendations made by most of the study groups derived from such an overview of education in the particular institution, and, to a considerable degree, the recommendations were intended to implement that overview. The matter to be considered is whether or not such reports can, in fact, provide a basis for responsible and relatively efficient action by large groups of highly individualistic faculty members. To illustrate the problem, consider the idea of a very considerable amount of freedom for the student in designing his academic program—an idea which is present in varying degrees in all the reports except Bell's. Since not all faculty members accept the basic idea of student freedom of choice, this proposition has to be considered on its own merits. If this is not done, many debates over specifics which are intended to implement that idea will not, in fact, be debates over the specifics but debates over the underlying concept. Discussion and debate in large groups are difficult under any conditions and not likely to be successful when the participants are not all dealing with the same issue. Second, all the study groups recognized that a lessening of curricular requirements calls for a strengthening of the academic advising or counseling process, since uniform requirements are, in a sense, simply a substitute for individual counseling. Thus a faculty that accepts the idea of greater student freedom in designing a curriculum must logically and responsibly accept the need for effective and available advising. This again demonstrates that before specific proposals for curriculum and advising are attacked, there must be discussion of, and some agreement about, the fundamental idea of student responsibility and choice. The proposals made in several reports for making residences more directly a part of the educational process are also a part of this matrix of freedom and

---

[7] *Education at Berkeley* was, compared with the others, much more ambivalent about its philosophy. Professor Pimental's minority report more fully states an educational philosophy for Berkeley. The fact that this latter was probably accepted by a large portion of the Berkeley faculty and that it had little to do with undergraduate education may explain the majority's reticence. (See also Martin Trow, "Bell, Book and Berkeley", *The American Behavioral Scientist,* May-June, 1968, pp. 43–48.)

guidance. There are many other examples in the reports of what a member of one group called "linked recommendations"—linked by common derivation from a basic educational concept or from a basic view of the particular institution. Both discussion and action are likely to be chaotic if the basic links are not generally accepted. Indeed, it will be recalled that many faculties voted to liberalize requirements without making a concomitant improvement in the advising system.

Such a requirement for ongoing discussion of basic educational concepts is probably impossible to meet in a group of any size, and especially a group with a legislative function. Most of the committees—not large groups—had stated that they avoided direct discussions of educational philosophy because they feared that such discussions would be endless and inconclusive. The committees, however, worked closely and long and were always able to review provisional decisions and to change them so that they would be part of a coherent whole. When one recalls that each of these studies involved several hundred—perhaps several thousand—man-hours, the idea of a faculty of several hundred or more persons going through the same process must be recognized as impossible.

The nub of the issue is the degree of change proposed. If the basic concepts of education and of the institution are pretty generally accepted and if the committee does not propose to change these in any fundamental way, the difficulty may not be so great. When fundamental change in objectives, structure, and process is proposed, the task may be impossible of accomplishment by the study-and-report technique. Most of the committees called for really fundamental change in the institution's basic posture as well as in details of teaching, advising, and curriculum. Too often, the latter were acted upon without the necessary acceptance of the former, and with such broad scope given to the committees, it is difficult to see how this could have been avoided.

LEADERSHIP    The cases indicate in both positive and negative ways that strong, skillful leadership is virtually mandatory for the success of any serious effort at educational reform. Faculty members have strong feelings of independence—ideological ones derived from the traditions of academia and supported by the tenure system and, increasingly, practical ones based on the relative independence from a particular institution which the contemporary mobile professor has.

The fierce jealousy with which academic departments guard their powers and prerogatives is well known to all observers of the academic scene. Less commonly commented upon is the increasing degree to which departmental power is abetted by professional accrediting agencies—external to, and largely independent of, the university. In most of the cases, colleges, schools, or other subunits, all with interests to defend, were also involved. All these individuals and groups have overlapping and conflicting interests and jurisdictions which are bound to be affected by changes in educational policies, and consequently the forces toward maintaining the *status quo* are enormous.

Given these conditions, a primary task of academic leadership is to try to counter the pressures favoring the *status quo* by creating or maintaining an atmosphere of receptivity to change. Individuals in several of the institutions considered here tried to lead in this direction, but unfortunately, the cases suggest that the approach they took—initiating major studies—is not a very good one. As was pointed out earlier, it does not seem possible to generate an atmosphere favorable to change through the study-and-report technique. Nevertheless, these men understood the need to overcome the inertia in a faculty. That the achievements of the studies were often marginal does not deny the leadership involved in starting them.

The greatest need for leadership and the greatest barrier to its effective exercise result from the complexity of the collegial process of decision making. The dispersion of power and status through the professor-department-college matrix means that the decision-making structure of most universities is remarkably flat in comparison with the structures found in business or government. A single individual—faculty member or administrator—will frequently find himself involved in a particular decision at three or more points through membership on several overlapping committees. There is no clear progression of issues through a hierarchy, and there are no sublevels at which the process of decision making may be controlled. To this must be added the fact that most of these reports made numerous and often interrelated recommendations, which simply complicated the process. A final complication is the keen sense, which most faculty members have, of the presence—real or imagined—of coercion or manipulation by the "administration."

Given the complexity of the typical university decision-making process and the pressures for the *status quo,* effective leadership in the consideration and implementation stages requires a keen sense of timing and priorities, an ability to keep things moving in an orderly fashion without appearing to force issues,[8] and above all, perhaps, bringing a shared sense of purpose to a disparate and individualistic group.

These elements of leadership were not greatly in evidence in most of the cases. Momentum was lost for one reason or another, wrong things were taken up at the wrong time, and debates were permitted to become contentious and irritating. Careful and detailed planning for consideration of these reports was not particularly evident anywhere except at Duke and Swarthmore. Some planning was done at Stanford, but other events—neither foreseeable nor controllable—interfered. Elsewhere, the lack of planning is an indication that those ostensibly in charge had simply not realized the complexity of what the institution was trying to do. No one was in charge of a situation that virtually demanded that someone assume a role of leadership.

Those instances where leadership did exist suggest that it does not necessarily have to come from the top. At Swarthmore, where the process was perhaps most effective, President Smith did lead—skillfully and effectively. But at Toronto, Dean Allen stepped into what had inadvertently become a leadership vacuum and brought about some sweeping changes. At Berkeley—a rather different situation—Professor Muscatine provided leadership when the report was introduced into the Academic Senate. At Brown, leadership was, at certain stages, exercised by an undergraduate student, Ira Magaziner.

Overall, the success of these efforts depends on some acceptance of the need for change before the study is started, and it requires leadership throughout the process, especially when a large number of sweeping proposals for change are to be acted upon by the community. Indeed, it may be only moderate oversimplification to suggest that leadership is the *sine qua non.* Even creating the nec-

---

[8] Faculty meetings are quite regularly described by participants as "hopeless messes," or worse. It has often occurred to me that an important qualification for a dean or president—even department chairmen in larger universities—is skill in running large meetings. After all, a good deal of a faculty's business is done in such meetings. Yet that particular qualification seems rarely to be considered. I have been a member of one "selection committee" and rather close to another, and I know that this particular qualification was never even considered, let alone evaluated. It seems reasonable to suggest that anyone moving into academic administration should acquire some training in this not very glamorous but terribly important aspect of the job.

essary atmosphere of hospitality to change when pressures to maintain the *status quo* are so great is itself a function of leadership.

While leadership is hard to come by in any circumstances, there is no reason to believe that universities do not have their share of it. What the universities do, however, is to circumscribe severely the possibilities for leaders to function. While I have suggested above that leadership involves keeping control over the whole difficult and complex process of decision making, it must be recognized that the collegial structure makes this unbelievably difficult. As David Riesman recently put it, "Democracy does take more time and leaves the administrator with decreasing leeway. . . . These [administrators] have minimal power and limited leverage over their departments, their students, their alumni, and their sources of financial and other public support."[9] The point is that in the process through which these studies have had to go, there are many points at which the faculty—or, more properly, small groups of faculty members—and, increasingly, students have the power to veto specific proposals for change, without accepting the requirement to propose responsible alternatives beyond maintenance of the *status quo*. Committee reports which really do communicate a "passion that moves men off their behinds" might overcome this built-in inertia, but the cases do not demonstrate that this is likely. What they do demonstrate is that leadership is vital and that the constraints on the exercise of leadership are many. They also demonstrate that in the absence of leadership, only overt pressure or the threat of it is likely to bring about change.

**INSTITU-TIONAL SIZE AND CHARACTER** While both Brown and Toronto made more sweeping changes, it is a reasonable conclusion that the *processes* of change were more nearly successful at Swarthmore than at the other institutions reviewed. Swarthmore is the smallest and the most homogeneous of all the institutions discussed here, and it is difficult, indeed, not to suspect that its success was related to this factor. Small size permits members of a community to get to know—perhaps to understand—one another and to learn to work together for common goals. Homogeneity permits the institution to have common goals—to develop a rather clear idea of what it is and what it wants to

[9] From "The Collision Course of Higher Education," an address given to the American Personnel and Guidance Association, March, 1969. I do not necessarily equate administrator with leader, although surely a good administrator is a leader.

become. Given these characteristics, it is much easier to decide that change is needed and to agree upon specific changes to be made. (There is a third aspect of institutional character, not much referred to in the cases, which is also of great importance: the availability of money. Fortunately, Swarthmore has that, too.)

Except where there was strong pressure from students, as at Brown and Toronto, the larger, more heterogeneous institutions were less able to bring about change, and again it is difficult not to conclude that there is a relationship. In varying degrees all these reports were trying to change institutions, and perhaps one of the insurmountable barriers to such change is the fact that these large, heterogeneous universities are less institutions than they are the various departments connected by a common plumbing system, as Robert Hutchins put it. It is quite obvious that we can have personnel policies and purchasing policies and library policies in any university, however large. All large bureaucracies have these. What is less obvious after examination of these studies is whether or not large institutions can have *educational* policies — whether the American tradition of giant institutions has not, in the case of higher education, reached the point of diminishing returns.

# 18. *The Limits of Collegiality*

The studies which formed the basis of this report were, in one way or another, responses to several striking and rapid developments in the general environment of higher education: the Academic Revolution, with its emphasis on professionalism and meritocracy; the knowledge explosion, which seems to be destroying confidence in the traditional, humane ideal of the educated man; the compound growth in the student population, which has brought with it so many qualitative changes as well as the obvious quantitative ones; and the rapid development of the student movement, with its challenges to the traditional values and structures underlying educational policy making. These environmental factors gave rise to the several educational policy issues with which the studies were concerned: teaching and advising, the nature of general education and the balance between it and specialized education, and the shifting to the academic departments of the balance of power in decisions about faculty and curriculum.

Judgments about the efficacy and soundness of any particular educational policies will inevitably be rather subjective, and the reader will surely form his own about those reported here. In the context of the extreme changes in the environment of higher education, the policy proposals, on the whole, strike me as being neither very imaginative nor very radical. Except to the extent that consideration of these studies has made several of the institutions more ready to change in the future,[1] the changes which have thus far

[1] Judgments about the effectiveness of the studies in creating conditions necessary for continuing and important change are also subjective. On every campus I visited I was referred to small groups or individuals who were doing "interesting and innovative things." Whether the studies, as opposed to other societal pressures for change, are responsible for these activities is not certain. Even less certain, I think, is the conclusion which some have drawn, that more widespread change will bubble up from these activities. I am not very sanguine about this because, as was pointed out in Chapter 16, real change in educational policy will require significant reallocation of resources, and at present, resource allocation is controlled for the most part by those who most benefit from the *status quo*.

resulted from the proposals seem, with some exceptions, to be only modest disturbances of the *status quo.*

Except for the student initiation of changes at Brown, all these proposals were developed and were acted upon collegially, so long the way in which the academy has conducted its business. Collegiality assumes that everyone in the community will have a voice in all its important decisions and that these decisions will reflect a broad base of acceptance. This, in turn, implies a general willingness to devote time and energy to the often tedious process of achieving such general acceptance. (Since it must also assume availability of time, it is clear that demands on time for participation in decision making must be relatively infrequent if other necessary work is to be done.) A still more basic assumption is that most of the faculty members are devoted primarily to the particular college or university and understand and accept its basic character, values, and goals. Collegiality as a system of self-government is well described by the term "community of scholars." Whether such communities have actually existed—at least in modern America—is beside the point. The model looms large in the rhetoric of the academy and was—ritualistically, at any rate—followed in all these studies.

Given the generally lackluster results of most of the studies, it is appropriate to ask whether or not we have reached the limits of collegiality as the basis for policy formulation—at least in the larger and more diverse institutions. The question was put in another way by David Truman during our discussion of Daniel Bell's study. He asked, "Can a faculty act like a faculty? Can it learn to take its collective responsibility for its curriculum and other matters?" The evidence from the studies is not reassuring on this point. It does suggest that we have passed the limits of collegiality as an effective system of decision making.

One limit on collegiality, one basis for a negative answer to Dr. Truman's question, is found in the proposals made by the studies and in the usual responses to them. For the most part, the changes which were proposed and generally accepted were largely those which would have little effect on the behavior patterns and value systems of most individual faculty members. Conversely, those areas where little concrete change was proposed, and even less generally accepted, were areas where professorial behavior patterns and value systems would have been significantly affected had consequential change occurred.

There seems, at this time, a consensus that such things as lessening requirements and student course loads, deemphasizing grades, and reducing the size of classes—all of which were proposed and generally accepted—have educational merit. It is also true that these are changes which can be made without much effect on what most faculty members do or on how they do it. Having general requirements makes more time available for the more narrowly specialized course offerings, which is the direction in which most curricula have been moving for some time. Reducing student course loads may not decrease faculty teaching loads, but it is highly unlikely that the latter will increase. Deemphasizing grades may well create problems in terms of graduate school admission processes, and it certainly bothers some faculty members who are much concerned about standards. Nevertheless, it is not likely to cause much of a change in the way one does one's teaching. As was suggested earlier, the desirability of small classes has always been an article of faith among most faculty members.

Conversely, if some of the problems of teaching, advising, and controlling the content and structure of education are indeed as great as several of the studies state them to be, it would be hard to deny educational merit to proposals intended to resolve them. Nevertheless, on the whole these matters were dealt with in a most tentative fashion. It is certain that making significant changes in teaching and advising would, above all, require a redirection and restructuring of what many professors do and of how much of their time is spent doing it. Departmental power has been built up largely through the efforts of professors in the departments, and to change this in any significant way would affect the behavior patterns of most faculty members. All in all, there is not much evidence in the proposals, or in the way in which they were generally received, to suggest that the essential element of collegiality—primary concern with the college or university and its character, values, and goals— was much in evidence. Other values and other goals seemed more compelling.

A second limit on collegiality is implicit in the structure of most universities in relation to their educational policies. Collegiality assumes a central focus for the institution which is shared by almost all its members. Yet on every campus I visited I was told by more than one person, "We are the most strongly departmentalized campus in the country." Apart from how this reflects on the validity of professorial statements, it does point to a condition which flies in the face of collegiality as the basis for policy making. An academic department can itself be collegial in nature, of course, and many no doubt are. But for as long as American undergraduate education places consequential limits on specialization (and all the studies reaffirmed these limits), collegiality, for the student, must transcend the department. The student's attention, effort, and allegiance will be directed toward an academic program which has roots throughout the college or university, and therefore planning and implementation of the program must be broadly based. To a considerable extent, the record of the cases indicates that this does not happen. As universities have grown larger and more heterogeneous and as faculties have become more a part of the department and of a national scholarly guild, as opposed to the central institution, the power of decision making has tended to move outward and to become more diffuse. It has become primarily a negative veto power which cannot be offset by the rhetoric of collegiality. And not surprisingly, the focus for planning and implementation has followed the power and ceased to be collegial in the institutional sense.

The studies and the consideration of them illustrate in still another way the limits of collegiality. While the degree of comprehensiveness varied, each study called for a review of the basic goals and objectives of the institution. The committees themselves did not face these issues directly, but came at them indirectly through long consideration of many related policy matters. The record of the cases makes quite clear that, for the most part, faculties never confronted these basic questions about goals and objectives at all. They failed to do so, in part, because the process of consideration was never structured so as to require them to. They failed to do so because it was simply not possible for them to take the amount of time the task required. Beyond these matters is the question of whether or not such large numbers of people—each with an equal voice—could be brought to face such fundamental issues in a productive way, even if structure and time were provided. Given the extreme diversity of interests and activity of these faculty members and their varying degrees of attachment to their particular institutions, it is not surprising that the collegial system has not, in these cases, worked very well.

It seems, then, that few of the conditions necessary for the effective functioning of a collegial system were present in these cases, even though the studies were carried on within that framework. Institutional size and diversity, which have resulted in the political and philosophical fragmentation of the institutions, undermine collegiality. So do the essentially pluralistic careers and loyalties of faculty members. All these prevented leadership—necessary even in a collegial system—from functioning.

If we have reached the limits of collegiality, there are two obvious patterns for a solution to the problem of policy making. One is to attempt to re-create the conditions which permit a collegial system to function. The other is to accept the fact that some institutions are not, and cannot be, collegial and to search for new ways of decision making in such institutions.

The relative success of the collegial process at Swarthmore suggests that it can work effectively in institutions which are neither too large nor too diverse and where the character and objectives of an institution are relatively well understood and accepted by its members. Obviously, we cannot create thousands of Swarthmores across the country. The masonry monuments to the educational ideas of previous generations which cover our campuses are not going to be abandoned or moved. But the several moves toward cluster colleges and satellite colleges which are under way around the country surely should be encouraged. New institutions—Santa Cruz or Hampshire, for example—can readily develop in ways which support collegiality. Buffalo's example suggests that an expanding institution can channel its growth through small, relatively homogeneous units. Michigan State has created such units in an institution which is neither new nor any longer expanding rapidly. In short, situations in which collegiality is a viable system of decision making now exist and are regularly being brought into being. More should be encouraged, I believe.

Ultimately, however, the organizational and financial problems involved in any such wholesale restructuring of our educational institutions are surely enormous, and thus the essential issue raised by this study is the apparent need, in the foreseeable future, for a new basis for decision making in relatively large and diverse universities. The pressures for change in our era are unremitting and must be responded to with more dispatch and assurance than appear to have characterized most of these studies.

The answer to this problem lies, I suggest, in the development of a system akin to the responsible government of the parliamentary democracies. Utilizing such a system would give recognition to the fact that after appropriate consultation, someone must have the power to make decisions. It would also take into account the fact that those who have the power must be responsible to those who are affected by the decisions for the way in which the power is used. This responsibility would be established by processes through which those who are affected can select the person or persons to whom the power of decision would be granted and can, with due cause, take back that power and transfer it to others. Specific arrangements would, of course, have to be made in light of the character and structure of any particular institution. (Such arrangements would have to include a definition of "those affected." In a broad sense, faculty, students, and those who provide material support are affected, but the extent to which each group is affected varies and some sort of weighting would generally be required.) Whatever the specific arrangements, their purpose would be to ensure ultimate control over the designated decision makers by all members of the university, while eliminating the latter's power to make decisions or, as is more frequently the case, to prevent decisions from being made.

Spiritually and philosophically, the attempt to re-create appropriate conditions for collegiality is attractive to me, although I recognize that large and diverse institutions have positive virtues as long as they can be made to function effectively. Furthermore, it seems foolish indeed to believe that conditions suitable for collegiality can be brought about in the short time which the pressures for change seem to permit us. At the moment, large and diverse institutions seem inevitable in our society. They can remain viable only through the self-discipline involved in accepting the necessity for the responsible use of power.

# Commentary

*Change in Educational Policy* is like the first part of a continued story—one wants to know what is going to happen next in the 11 colleges and universities whose policy studies are reported by Mr. Ladd, and particularly one wants to know what will happen in the 9 colleges and universities studied intensively.

This study of studies cries for a reappraisal in five or ten years, even though it must of course be recognized that other forces in any future period will be impinging on the colleges and universities of this group to create new changes and that the effect of the original self-study would be difficult to tease out.

It should also be recognized that the universe represented by these colleges and universities—Berkeley, New Hampshire, Toronto (in Canada as the exception to the United States studies), Swarthmore, Wesleyan, Michigan State, Duke, Brown, and Stanford—is by no means representative of higher education in the United States. Mr. Ladd does not present the group as a scientifically drawn sample, but he does consider the institutions included "typical" of four-year programs. I should disagree to some extent, for I consider them typical of the better institution only, but if I could put my money on a larger study of a more representative group or a later restudy of the same group, I should choose the second as the more likely source of vital information.

Mr. Ladd raises some fundamental questions. The most basic is clearly that taken up explicitly in the last chapter, "The Limits of Collegiality." Collegiality as a system of self-government is considered by Mr. Ladd to be well described by the term "community of scholars," whether or not such communities actually exist. The important questions from the point of view of this area of discussion are whether everyone in the community has a voice, whether decisions reflect a broad base of acceptance—and so by implication

a working measure of consensus on the goals of the institution—
and whether there is willing and competent manpower to implement the decisions for change. Mr. Ladd concludes that we have
passed the limits of collegiality as an effective system of decision
making.

Mr. Ladd's proposals are that conditions that permit a collegial
system to function be created—as, for example, this functioned at
Swarthmore and presumably has or could at many other small
institutions or large ones with successful centers dividing the whole
into smaller units—or that a "system akin to the responsible government of the parliamentary democracies" be adopted, based on the
appropriate consultations and then the delegation of authority to
someone to make decisions. In this connection one thinks of King-
man Brewster's argument, not for wider representation in college
governance, but for more clear-cut arrangements for review of the
work of those who have the authority to make decisions and of the
accountability of those persons.

The studies almost all confine themselves to undergraduate
education, not because graduate education does not need reconsideration, but because most had the opinion that was found in
Mr. Ladd's own institution, New Hampshire, that the "undergraduate student body is that part of the university community
most demanding of attention at the minute." Within undergraduate
education most studies concentrate more on basic education, whatever it is called, than on the major. They reflect an interest in
"loosening" the curricular requirements, in the students' terms,
greater flexibility. The emphasis seems to have swung back to
greater freedom of choice among courses and departments, the
choice often to include advanced courses. The swing "back" in this
case is away from general education, which received such impetus
from the Harvard *Redbook* of 1945, with Bell of Columbia the only
strong voice in favor of an extended general education program.[1]

The "new" freedom includes independent study, which no one
presents as new but only as more important, and "project work,"
which is probably different from the field work of earlier days
chiefly in that it is more prominent in some of the institutions and
is also more likely to be originated by students.

[1] In relation to the *Redbook,* "General Education in a Free Society," Mr. Ladd
expresses the opinion that ". . . most Americans [1945] showed an optimistic
confidence that American society was, and would continue to be, free and
viable."

Class size is clearly important to many study groups, with two overall objectives related to it. The first is to give students early in their college experience close contact with at least a few faculty members through small classes, seminars, tutorials, independent study, etc. The second and related objective is to provide students an opportunity to get discussions started not only with faculty members but among themselves—discussions, it is hoped, they would continue on their own. Changes along these lines would mean greater demands on faculty time, but there are thought to be compensating factors in the reduction of course load for students, and so directly or indirectly of faculty load.

Greater demands on faculty time than any caused by changes in class size or teaching arrangements would be the result of the frequently raised, but certainly not settled or well-structured, recommendation for more extensive student advising. It is recognized in almost all studies that greater flexibility for students in choosing their programs requires advising by somebody, and the recommendations of the institutions in this group range from more time for "professional" counselors (Michigan State), through various arrangements for more advising by faculty members, to the informal association of faculty and students in residence halls.[2] Related to the recommendation for greater contact between students and faculty members or other designated persons, whether through teaching or advising, is the recognition that many students seem to be searching for a more personal relationship with their mentors, to use a convenient word the students would not be likely to use.

Both small classes, despite compensating factors, and increased time for advising students would require larger expenditures. The "charges" to the self-study committee had nothing to do with the finances of the institution; the committees were not held down to projecting cost estimates. Consequently, while the power of the purse was recognized in relation to the authority of the officer or committee in charge of instituting changes, the hard choices likely to have to be made for institutional or even divisional or departmental budgets were not part of the studies. In this connection I find again an argument for repeating the study with an effort to discover how changes were paid for, and specifically whether by

[2] Only Stanford recommends making an extra payment to faculty members for advising 15 or more freshman ($500 a year) or providing research assistance to faculty members advising 15 or more upperclassmen.

new sources of money or by rechanneling money earlier budgeted for different programs.

Matters of widespread interest included the ways in which students' achievement was recorded—numerical grade; pass-fail or some variation thereof, including a "pass-erase" reported for Stanford; no grade at all for the first term; or descriptive comments instead of grades. Dissatisfaction with grading, like dissatisfaction with teaching and with advising, was evident pretty nearly universally. The calendar, too, came in for suggested reforms, but without a clear choice among the institutions, nor probably among the disciplines within an institution.

I note the dissatisfaction with teaching, and I should emphasize strongly that it goes beyond the nature of the curriculum and directly to the quality of the teaching often found in the first year or two of the student's work. The vehemence with which many critics set up research as the enemy of teaching is lacking in these self-studies and in Mr. Ladd's analysis, but it is repeatedly made clear that the rewards of research—both in terms of the faculty member's own satisfaction and in terms of his academic advancement—weigh more heavily than the rewards of teaching. It is recommended, of course, that teaching be given greater weight by those concerned with promotion and tenure, but no study group seems to have found ways to assure that this recommendation will go further than the text of the committee report. External factors such as "teacher of the year" awards seem trivial in relation to the magnitude of the problem.

The advantages and disadvantages of teaching assistants are also evaluated, particularly, of course, in the very large institutions, where they do such a substantial percentage of the teaching. Unequivocal recommendations would of course run into difficulty, for example, the recommendation that all graduate students (or all Ph.D. candidates) have one year as a teaching assistant. It would probably be the experience of every institution that some Ph.D. candidates who stand very high in their competence in research are failures as teaching assistants. Senior faculty members can also be urged to teach the teaching assistants to teach, but some would find it more satisfactory to teach the undergraduate students themselves. That choice would be fine if the teaching were done with the same care and vigor the senior faculty members invest in the teaching of research assistants.

In short, there are no easy answers when the quality of teaching is the question, and perhaps the most relevant step most of the studies would advocate—though not primarily for this reason—is the greater freedom recommended by everyone but Bell to undergraduates to make their own choices, to develop their own programs.

The studies are analyzed for "process" as well as "content," and the process part of the analysis will be of great interest to anyone who plans to direct or to take an active part in a self-study.[3] Overall, one cannot help being impressed by the part fate plays in many of them—the death or departure of a key person, unexpected support by new individuals or groups, etc. It is evident that the director or directing committee has to be ready to land on his or its feet when the unexpected requires a new start.

Mr. Ladd, in his analysis and through the very different processes of the studies, shows some of the major requirements, not all of them likely to be present in any one study: readiness for study, even if not for change; leadership; sufficient manpower, including some instances where most of the manpower seemed to consist of senior faculty members, others where junior faculty members became involved, and the striking instance at Brown where students were leaders as well as manpower; the decision whether or not to include outside examiners; advance assurance of publication, as at Swarthmore; and overturned customs, like the week of canceled classes at Swarthmore with a variety of meetings to concentrate on the published study and the 2 ½-day faculty meeting at Brown with large numbers attending.[4]

A preliminary part of the process which might have been expected —consideration of educational philosophy, of the goals of the institution, or more specifically of the undergraduate program— Mr. Ladd found rarely present. It seems that the committees and the faculties took off in terms of educational policy. Mr. Ladd

[3] Mr. Ladd makes no comparison between these self-studies and those prepared for the regional accrediting associations, although there are both differences and similarities which might throw some light on the possible process.

[4] On the subject of manpower it should be noted that most of the studies began before students became interested in the governance of the university and taking an active part in developing its work. Many students joined up as the studies proceeded. Brown was the notable exception in that the students' sense of urgency preceded that of the faculty.

A further point of interest on manpower is Mr. Ladd's report that only two women were included in the study committees, the dean of Pembroke *ex officio* and an "outside" member at Swarthmore. Committee lists, not given for all institutions, show one other woman, a graduate student at Stanford.

judges the policy proposals to be neither very radical nor very imaginative. He is critical of them also for a different reason — because they rarely challenge the authority of the departments or the attitudes of faculty members, especially in the areas where challenge would hurt most, the major and the teaching of advanced students and graduate students. Some faculty members reporting to him expressed the opinion that the initial changes would create a situation in which further changes would "bubble up." Whether this develops is of course an open question for the future.

Mr. Ladd is more inclined than I to find similarities between institutions in both content and process (the same general problems and the same solutions). I am struck by the differences, and I think it is from these differences that we can learn most for future studies. Radical or imaginative proposals might add to the possibility of learning, but right here in this limited group of institutions there are not only sobering thoughts for new work but very clear-cut indications of what might succeed in meeting desired ends under given conditions.

*Katharine E. McBride*

# References

**Bell, Daniel:** *The Reforming of General Education: The Columbia College Experience in Its National Setting,* Columbia University Press, New York, 1966.

**Berk.:** See Select Committee on Education: *Education at Berkeley,* Academic Senate, University of California, Berkeley, March, 1966.

**Br.:** See Special Committee on Educational Principles: *Interim Report and Recommendations,* Brown University, April, 1969.

**Caplow, Theodore, and Reece J. McGee:** *The Academic Marketplace,* Basic Books, Inc., Publishers, New York, 1958; Anchor Books, Garden City, N.Y., 1965.

**Duke:** See Subcommittee on Curriculum: *Varieties of Learning Experience,* Undergraduate Faculty Council, Duke University, March, 1968.

**Faculty of Swarthmore College:** *An Adventure in Education,* Swarthmore, Pa., 1942.

**Heiss, Ann:** *Study of Graduate Education in 10 Graduate Institutions,* Center for Research and Development in Higher Education, University of California, Berkeley, 1969.

**Jencks, Christopher, and David Riesman:** *The Academic Revolution,* Doubleday & Company, Inc., Garden City, N.Y., 1968.

**MS:** See Committee on Undergraduate Education: *Improving Undergraduate Education,* Michigan State University, October, 1967.

**NH:** See University-wide Educational Policies Committee: *Toward Unity from Diversity,* University of New Hampshire, February, 1967.

**Riesman, David:** "The Academic Procession," *Constraint and Variety in American Education,* University of Nebraska Press, Lincoln, 1956.

**Riesman, David:** "The Collision Course of Higher Education," an address given to the American Personnel and Guidance Association, March, 1969.

Rudolph, Frederick: *The American College and University,* Vintage Books, New York, 1965.

Stan.: See Steering Committee of the Study of Education at Stanford: *Study of Education at Stanford,* Stanford University, November, 1968, *et seq.*

SW.: See Commission on Educational Policy: *Critique of a College,* Swarthmore College, November, 1967.

Tor.: See Presidential Advisory Committee on Undergraduate Instruction: *Undergraduate Instruction in Arts and Sciences,* Faculty of Arts and Sciences, University of Toronto, July, 1967.

Trow, Martin: "Bell, Book and Berkeley," *The American Behavioral Scientist,* May-June, 1968, pp. 43–48.

UCLA: See Committee on Academic Innovation and Development: *Report,* Academic Senate, University of California, Los Angeles, November, 1967.

Vesey, Laurence R.: *The Emergence of the American University,* The University of Chicago Press, Chicago, 1965.

Wes.: See *The Study of Educational Policies and Programs at Wesleyan,* Wesleyan University, May, 1968.

# Acknowledgments

My obligations are many: to the dozens of faculty members, administrative officers, and students who talked with me cordially and with candor, thus providing the essential substance of this study; to Clark Kerr, who saw the possibilities in such a study and made available essential support from the Carnegie Commission; to David Riesman, who helped me in the initial stages and read and commented upon early drafts; to my colleague Herman Gadon, who also read, criticized, and at a crucial moment gave assurance; to my dean, Jan E. Clee, whose administrative philosophy is to make it possible for each person to do his own thing; to Mrs. Clare Constance and Mrs. Marilyn Bock, who cheerfully and capably typed and typed; and to my wife, whose keen eye for grammatical and syntactical lapses will surely ease the reader's task and whose help has, in so many ways, eased mine.

I have a special and long-standing obligation to my nine colleagues on the University-wide Educational Policies Committee of the University of New Hampshire, who taught me so much about higher education and who demonstrated that the ideological, professional, and personal barriers that so often divide men in academia can be overcome.

*Dwight R. Ladd*

# Index